Praise for
From Tweens to Teens

"*From Tweens to Teens: The Parents' Guide to Preparing Girls for Adolescence* by Maria Clark Fleshood is a must-read book for all parents who want to understand and support their daughters' journey to finding their identity,strengths and potential. Inspiring and illuminating, Maria Fleshood's book teaches parents how to use rituals to gain self-efficacy and self-confidence as they move into adolescence. This book is a gift for the whole family and the culture at large."

—JETTE SIMON, Clinical Psychologist (DK-Degree),
Director of Washington, DC, Training Institute for Couples Therapy

"Maria Fleshood gives her readers, both clinicians and parents of growing girls, some exceptional tools in her much-needed book. Touching both head and heart, she does so with the hands-on skills of a solid, experienced therapist. Her research into scholarly studies provides a sound theoretical basis for her direction. Her case studies show not only the effectiveness of the rituals but also her heart of compassion contained in this approach. She does all this without excessive sentimentality, although the reader may be moved to tears by a few of the cases. This guide is most timely for the current generation of parents and grandparents who want the best for their girls but who are overwhelmed by the technological world of today's kids and the seeming power those smart phones/social groups have. I recommend this book not only for therapists, parents, and grandparents but also the many others who are trying to be helpful to girls growing into adolescence in this world that has lost most of the transitional rituals of our ancestors in all cultures."

—G. KEITH PARKER, PhD, Pastoral Counselor and Jungian Analyst

"Dr. Fleshood's book provides parents with the integrative information, framework, and tools they need to help their daughters develop a strong core of identity, have the courage to hold onto their values, and the fortitude to develop the inner resources they need to cope with life now and in the future. At some point, we know that we will have to trust our children to make the right choices in life on their own. Dr. Fleshood's book provides the guide parents need to prepare their daughters for when that day comes. It's a must read and an invaluable resource for parents raising girls."

—LISA ZOPPETTI, PhD Clinical Psychologist and
mother of tween and teen girls

"*From Tweens to Teens: The Parents' Guide to Preparing Girls for Adolescence* provides readers with insight and guidance in the creative use of shared rituals to support young girls through their developmental passages into healthy adolescence. A master therapist, Maria Clark Fleshood introduces readers to the wisdom of ritual in support of contemporary parenting. Her writing is scholarly, accessible, and filled with the joy of life, making this a must-read."

—PAULA RAY, PsyD, Pediatric Neuropsychologist

"Through our work with Dr. Fleshood, we have established many meaningful family traditions. A family favorite has become the 'memory box.' Family members including grandparents, aunts, uncles and cousins are asked to give the high school graduate a special 'memento' to commemorate a treasured memory. The box of mementos is intended to provide the graduate with love and support when perhaps homesickness or challenging times arise. The outpouring of love demonstrated during this tradition has helped our family develop stronger relationships with one another."

—MARC W. FLICKINGER, MD

FROM
Tweens
TO Teens

FAMILIUS

Published by Familius LLC, www.familius.com

Familius books are available at special discounts for bulk purchases, whether for sales promotions or for family or corporate use. For more information, contact Familius Sales at 559-876-2170 or email orders@familius.com.

Library of Congress Cataloging-in-Publication Data
2015956719

Paperback ISBN 9781942934561
Ebook ISBN 9781942934981
Hardcover ISBN 9781942934998

Printed in the United States of America

Edited by Katharine Hale
Cover design by David Miles
Book design by Brooke Jorden

10 9 8 7 6 5 4 3 2 1

First Edition

FROM
Tweens
TO Teens

**THE PARENTS' GUIDE
TO PREPARING GIRLS
FOR ADOLESCENCE**

MARIA CLARK FLESHOOD

To my children, Beth and Phillip, for the abundant joy, love, and laughter you offer to parenthood.

In memory of my mother, Ercell Elizabeth Potter, for modeling unconditional love and acceptance throughout my childhood.

Contents

Preface xi

Introduction 1

Part I: Understanding Adolescence 5

Chapter 1: A Complex Age 9

Chapter 2: Seeking Connection 15

Chapter 3: Why Rituals? 21

Part II: Rituals for All Ages 29

Chapter 4: Getting Started 33

Chapter 5: Ritual One: Separation, Age Eight 35

Chapter 6: Ritual Two: Letting Go, Age Nine 47

Chapter 7: Ritual Three: Making Wise Connections, Age Ten 57

Chapter 8: Ritual Four: Staying Connected, Age Eleven 69

Chapter 9: Ritual Five: Dropping Inside, Age Twelve 85

Chapter 10: Ritual Six: The Return, Age Thirteen 99

Part III: What Comes Next? 113

Chapter 11: It's Never Too Late 117

Chapter 12: Seeing Through a New Lens 129

Appendix 135

Notes 139

Bibliography 143

Preface

Lisa, a seventeen-year-old high school student, sat in my counseling office, head bowed, voice trembling in anger and heartbreak. "I really believed I was something back then," she said, describing herself at eight years old. "You know—important, like everyone really cared about what I had to say and who I was. Where did *I* go? Where I am really sucks, and I hate myself; I hate my life."

What happens to happy, energetic pre-puberty girls that they so often lose themselves during their adolescent years? In the crucial bridging from girlhood into young womanhood, adolescent females often struggle to hold on to their assertive, secure, and courageous selves that defined their formative years.

Having worked for more than thirty years as an educator and clinical psychotherapist with female adolescents and their families, I have met a lot of Lisas. These young women have profoundly shaped my personal and professional conviction that the adolescent years do not have to be such a trying time for girls or their families. It can—and should—be different.

This book evolved out of my doctoral project, "Reviving Rites of Passage for Adolescent Girls," in which I worked with six high school girls and their parents for a year, guiding the girls and their parents through six stages of a rite of passage. I wrote *From Tweens to Teens: The Parents' Guide to Preparing Girls for Adolescence* out of a sense of urgency for parents to understand the physiological and psychological needs of daughters entering adolescence. The in-between years are the time for parents to help their daughters create an internal framework to support an identity that is not based on the shallow hype that the media and other external forces promote. By providing parents with developmental information and a step-by-step process to incorporate age-relevant rituals into their daughters' lives, I wanted to offer a new paradigm that, when implemented, allows families to experience positivity and connection.

From Tweens to Teens provides educational information, parenting skills, and powerful vignettes that teach parents how to mark the years between childhood and adolescence with meaningful rituals that support their daughters as they cross this developmental divide.

There are vision-quest weekends, clinical workshops, and camps that teach the psychological necessity of a rite of passage and offer this experience to adolescents. Although good and valuable to those who participate, they often are costly, require extensive travel, and fail to involve the immediate family. My goal in this book is to help more parents learn how to implement rituals within the family throughout their daughters' preteen years, strengthening the most influential relationships in a young girl's life.

I have seen the results of these rituals in the lives of hundreds of girls and parents who have used them over the years. My hope is that many more families can experience the richness and connection these rituals offer.

Introduction

A few years ago, while riding in the car with my three granddaughters, ages nine, eight, and five, I was amused as they began singing along with a female pop star. "Turn it up, Grammy," the five-year-old said. "We love this song. It rocks!"

At first, I thought it was fun and entertaining. As I listened with more attention to the lyrics, my opinion changed. All three girls were singing at the top of their lungs, not missing a word or beat as they carried the tune until its final note.

When we arrived home, I asked my granddaughters why they liked that song. Out of the mouths of babes: Halee, the eight-year-old, said, "It's just cool and fun to sing. And anyway, Grammy, Katy Perry is so sexy."

"Oh, 'sexy,'" I said. "Why do you think she is sexy?"

The youngest, Libby, rolled her eyes in disbelief. "Grammy, don't you know what sexy is? Just wait, and we'll show you."

The three girls ran upstairs and pulled out clothes from their suitcases and the dress-up box I keep for them. An hour or so went by as my husband and I waited for the announced performance.

Emmy—the oldest—started downstairs, Perry's performance of the superhit "E.T." blasting from her iPod. The girls made their way down the stairs, singing into pretend microphones they had crafted out of construction paper. Dressed in colorful costumes with necklines pulled down and shoulders exposed from T-shirts stretched to one side, the three bodies moved with such seductive ease that their translation of "sexy" made even these fairly open-minded grandparents stiffen.

Later that evening, I peeked into their room to find three girls transformed. Wearing PJs, they were holding their soft bed buddies to their necks as they settled into a deep slumber. I leaned against the frame of their bedroom door for a few moments, thinking how easy it is for girls this age to slip back and forth over the fragile, thin line that gently—and sometimes not-so-gently—separates the innocence of their girlhood from the challenges of their teen years.

Listening to my granddaughters singing about being taken, wanting to be a victim, and being willing to be abducted, I could not ignore how closely this catchy tune mirrors the behavior of ten-, eleven-, and twelve-year-old girls who surrender themselves emotionally and sexually only to feel victimized by the very ones who promised to make them feel special forever.

Several weeks later, I was just wrapping up my work for the day when I received a phone call from the mother of a client with whom I had recently started working. The mother's voice trembled as she struggled to tell me that her thirteen-year-old daughter was in the hospital, fighting for her life.

Heather—a beautiful, vibrant girl—was struggling to survive an overdose of Tylenol PM. After discovering via Facebook that the friend to whom she had surrendered her innocence had decided she no longer needed Heather's friendship or the love affair they had recently entered, Heather made a choice that life was no longer worth her effort. Twenty pills later, the secret was out and Heather was facing a battle she wasn't sure she wanted to win—one her family had had no idea existed.

Shortly after my conversation with Heather's mom, I found myself reaching for a favorite quote I often read to parents who struggle to stabilize the difficult and narrow passage their daughters take into adolescence. Somehow, in this moment, it felt right to sit with the words English poet David Whyte thought as he paused to watch his daughter while she slept. I heard Whyte speak at the 2009 Psychotherapy Networker Symposium in Washington, DC. His words have stayed with me since—particularly at times like this when I'm seeking to help parents navigate their daughters' teen years:

She will be called into a thousand voices other than her own. Far too long, girls in our culture have been turning away from their birthright of aliveness, joyfulness, and completeness. This time is a golden opportunity for parents to capture and guide their daughters to pursue their desires and trust their wisdoms before they are infiltrated with external role models who will exile them from their truest selves.[1]

As I made my way home, my mind seemed to weave between the words Whyte wrote to his daughter and the lyrics Perry sang to her alien, futuristic lover, each offering opposing directions for girls in their search for completeness, love, and acceptance.

My mind drifted back to three innocent girls role-playing "sexy" while singing about being taken away, taken over, and led into the light—where a girl would risk anything to feel powerful and special. For Heather, the exile from self that Whyte spoke of had happened, and the voices of external forces had won—at least momentarily.

It doesn't have to be that way. Would Heather's story have played out differently if she had arrived at the most challenging years of life believing from within that she was worthy, liked, loved, and special? Unfortunately, we will never know, as neither Heather nor her parents can rewind and redo those years. However, new chapters have been added to Heather's story—chapters that show a family shifting from surviving adolescence to thriving. Learning how to stay connected in the midst of tensions that often rupture relationships during these years has brought healing and hope to a family who came very close to the edge.

From Tweens to Teens: The Parents' Guide to Preparing Girls for Adolescence invites parents to rethink how they guide and prepare their daughters to face their most difficult developmental years. The majority of parents with whom I work are eager to know how to help their daughters navigate these years but struggle with understanding how. This book provides parents with tools to build their daughter's self-esteem from the inside out, not leaving her dependent on outside voices to define her. In helping to strengthen your daughter's inner world, you empower her to successfully face and move through her outer world.

In this book, you will learn a six-step methodology of rituals, beginning when your daughter is eight years old and ending when she is thirteen. These rituals, inspired by traditional coming-of-age ceremonies from around the world, will strengthen family ties and remind young girls that they are not alone in this journey from pre-teen to young woman. These rituals will support you and empower her as each of you journeys through these years.

PART I: Understanding Adolescence

As girls step into the crossroads between girlhood and womanhood, they stop asking "Who am I and what do I want?" and instead ask "Who can I please and how can I do that?" The seeds of confidence and independence planted by parents and community are now challenged by peers, social networking, and media images. Often without notice, girls' confident and courageous voices become silent, replaced with self-doubt and fear of rejection.

Adolescence will never be absent of chaotic mood swings, increased irritability, and sensitivity to emotions. Due to the increased developmental activity of the adolescent brain, behaviors will shift in a second. The biological shifts and the external pressures girls encounter as they begin to separate from what has been familiar and move toward independence influence temperaments and evoke tensions at home. This is natural, normal, and necessary.

What I want parents to trust is that although brain development has a significant impact on your daughter's behavior during these years, your presence and commitment to her journey is by far the most valuable asset to the success of her development. The assumption that hormones have more power over your daughter's teen years than you is simply not true—it never has been. Learning how to navigate through this important time in your daughter's life by understanding the significance of rituals and adopting them into your lives is an opportunity to help your daughter transition into young womanhood, resulting in a smoother ride for parent and child.

Chapter 1

A Complex Age

The struggles of girls to survive adolescence have not gone unnoticed. For decades, experts on female development have studied this population to understand why girls in the United States have such difficulty at this stage of their lives.

As early as 1928, American anthropologist Margaret Mead questioned whether nature or nurture played a more dominant role in dictating the problems that seemed to define adolescence in the United States. In her research among Samoan girls, Mead sought to answer her primary questions: "Are the disturbances which vex our adolescents due to the nature of adolescence itself or to the civilisation [that raises them]? Under different conditions does adolescence present a different picture?"[1] In her conclusion, Mead writes, "The passage from childhood to adulthood—adolescence—in Samoa was a smooth transition and not marked by the emotional or psychological distress, anxiety, or confusion seen in the United States."[2] She came to believe that the paradigm that resulted in the emotional stress and turmoil of female adolescents here could be—and needed to be—different.

Six decades later, Carol Gilligan reported on her research into the unique problems faced by adolescent girls in the United States when they step into their teen years. She also argued that the paradigm should be different. Gilligan and colleagues Annie Rogers and Deborah Tolman point to the "social pressures that silence girls rather than empower them to pursue their goals and learn to heed their own voices."[3]

On the heels of Gilligan's research, Mary Pipher rang the same alarm in her bestselling book *Reviving Ophelia: Saving the Selves of Adolescent Girls.* She challenged society to take seriously the power of negative and abusive cultural messages that shape the most crucial years of girls' development. She writes, "Something dramatic happens to girls in early adolescence. Just as planes and ships disappear mysteriously in the Bermuda Triangle, so do the selves of girls go down in droves. They crash and burn in a social and developmental Bermuda Triangle."[4]

In my clinical work, I sit with young girls every week who give voice to this crash. Some come very close to not surviving the burn. Due to less face-to-face contact with their parents, communication between them is at an all-time low, leaving girls estranged from a vital connection they desperately need. As a result, girls end up feeling alone, with no guide to help them work through fears, self-doubt, and insecurities. Girls I work with report they are unhappy with and worried about their body image and their academic and social performance. In their struggle for acceptance, they commonly surrender to sex, alcohol, or drugs. To relieve the guilt and hopelessness these bring, girls increasingly are turning to cutting and other forms of self-harm. In their darkest hour, some girls—like Heather, whose story will be examined further in Chapter 2—attempt suicide.

In her article "Teen Depression—Girls: How to Get Closer to

Your Teenaged Daughter and Prevent Depression," Ellen McGrath reports, "By any measure, our young people are in trouble. Rates of depression and anxiety are soaring—and getting worse. Possibly one out of three [teen girls] will end up with significant clinical depression needing treatment. Their suicide rates have tripled." McGrath goes on to discuss the reasons for rampant depression among teens:

> [Teens] face unprecedented pressures to succeed. . . . As the pressure has increased, so has anxiety, because adults aren't there to teach kids how to handle it. It's exploding in eating disorders, anxiety disorders and aggression. This is the first generation of divorce, the product of absentee parents and lots of conflict. Today's teens face more pressure for sexual activity earlier, a situation that can be very depressing for those who aren't ready or don't know what to do. There is an epidemic of low self-esteem, because parents haven't had the time it takes to build it. That has left adolescent girls prey to body image issues.[5]

As McGrath points out, teen girls do not know what to do with the stress they encounter. They are not psychologically prepared or physically ready to deal with the social pressures and demands that confront them during their teen years. Far too early in their lives, they are faced with a more dangerous, sexualized, and cyber-saturated culture than ever before. As a result, they become overwhelmed and try to overcompensate for their inability to handle the inappropriate stress these pressures add to their lives.

The Committee on Adolescence of the American Academy of Pediatrics reported in 2007 that "[t]he number of adolescent deaths that result from suicide in the United States ha[s] been increasing dramatically during recent decades. . . . Suicide is the third leading cause of death for adolescents fifteen to nineteen years old."[6] The problem was given national attention when CBS News reported that according to numbers released by the Centers for Disease Control and Prevention, the suicide rate rose 8 percent among young people ages ten to twenty-four from 2003 to 2004—the biggest bump in fifteen years—in what one official called "'a dramatic and huge increase.' . . . The biggest increase—about 76 percent—was in the suicide rate for ten- to fourteen-year-old girls. . . . Suicide rates among older teen girls, those aged fifteen to nineteen, shot up 32 percent."[7]

Experts agree about the intense pressures teen girls face and their horrific results. McGrath urges, "We need to take action."[8] Pipher argued for building a society that offers a healthy environment for girls as they move through their teen years.[9] But how many times do the alarms need to sound? How many decades must go by before young girls are liberated from the abusive paradigm that has made their teen years stressed filled and chaotic for both parent and child?

We do need to take action. We need to build a new society that prepares and empowers girls to flourish during their teen years rather than drown. Girls need a society that models self-respect, encourages independent thinking, and validates their efforts to speak up rather than silencing them. But if we look closely at the ways in which cultural norms have influenced and shaped the image girls develop today, it is obvious that our culture is still ill equipped to build a safe foundation on which girls can individuate, actualize, and thrive.

This was made painfully clear by a *USA Today* article by Maria Puente, "From the Sandbox to the Spa," about the exploding trend of beauty and spa treatments for young girls. "The size of the child consumer pool (ages five to nineteen) is an estimated 61 million, according to the US Census, and is projected to rise to 81 million by 2050. So it's no surprise that the spa and beauty industries view them as a not-fully-tapped market that could sustain their business for decades."[10]

In 2011, *The Week* published a report about geoGirl, "a new line of 69 cosmetics products, from blush and mascara to exfoliators, aimed at the tween market. It's designed especially for young girls who want to use 'real cosmetics, but with natural ingredients,' says Joel Carden of Pacific World, the line's manufacturer."[11]

Marketing this product to young girls is seductive. It comes disguised as the retailer's concern for parents and young girls who want to use cosmetics with natural ingredients, but it is far more likely that the retailer's intent is to make money off the pressure on preteens to look pretty and perfect. This only adds to the concern over girls measuring their self-worth based on what is on the outside.

Makeover parties for kids from kindergarten through third grade are now sponsored by elementary schools, and makeover diva birthday parties are on the rise for girls as young as five years old. A mother recently showed me a website she had found while searching for birthday ideas for her eight-year-old daughter that read: "Need inspiration for your daughters' guests? Ideal Beauty Themed Parties is your answer!" Is this how we invest in empowering young girls to discover and define what is ideal for them? Not if we want them to grow up prepared and empowered to enter the complex world that awaits them.

Marketers will not relinquish their hold of this population, but parents can loosen the tight grip these products have on their daughters' attention—and wallets. Daughters, granddaughters, and nieces do not have to be prisoners to cultural pressures and trends that dictate what "normal," "pretty," "smart," or "worthy" looks like. If girls are to be released from damaging pressures and social trends, a new response is needed from the culture—and it can start right inside a girl's home, as the following chapters show.

Chapter 2

Seeking Connection

ased on the analysis in the previous chapter, the situation for young girls may seem hopeless. I don't believe that, and neither should you. In fact, the work I have done with parents and daughters has taught me that this period does not have to be a stressful, dreadful time. You have the power to shape how these years unfold. The great challenge for all parents is how to face those moments that are unfamiliar, uncomfortable, and confusing.

Pain and isolation have become the norm for many young girls as they move into and through their adolescent years. Most girls desperately want acceptance but struggle to find it in a world that demands perfection and performance at almost any cost. Girls report spending hours daily re-creating themselves, getting it right on their online profile, and crafting their storyline in a virtual world that gives only the illusion that people "out there" are interested in and connected to them. They text thousands of messages a week to ensure they are wanted, popular, and good enough. Girls invest hours obsessing over their weight, modeling themselves after images in the media that project "thin is in" and "pretty is perfect."

The pattern of disavowing themselves that starts during the tween years can follow girls into adulthood. Many girls appear impressive and confident, and they easily convince parents, peers, and teachers they are fine. When we look beneath these projections, however, we often discover that these images are not congruent with the girls' belief systems that dictate how they respond in relationships.

Most parents want their daughters to be self-sufficient, confident, and happy, but knowing how to make that happen is where parents struggle. They feel powerless and bewildered and, out of desperation, surrender to the belief that they cannot influence the outcome. Some parents' greatest hope at this stage is to "just get through it."

In my clinical work with adolescent girls and parents, I have discovered that the most common motivator behind girls' willingness to surrender their values, desires, and opinions is the fear of rejection. Girls entering their teen years have a developmental need to feel validated and accepted by those around them. If they don't receive this from their parents, they are even more desperate to get it from other sources. If they have no anchor to remind them they matter, their confusion grows.

At this age perhaps more than any other, these girls need to feel connected. In this increasingly digitized world, girls have more contact with screens than with parents. Multitasking parents leave children competing for attention, never feeling connected or heard. Girls report that parents are physically close but mentally elsewhere. Texting has replaced talking, and scrolling through Twitter, emails, or Facebook updates interrupts time formerly used to share events of the day as families gathered around the table to eat or play games.

The face-to-face human connection that girls crave and need as they prepare for and enter their teen years has diminished. Left without a connection to the most important role models in their lives, young girls turn to outsiders for attention and validation to fulfill their need to be seen.

I do not begin to suggest that you pull the plug on your daughter's cell phone, iPod, computer, or other media connections, nor do you need to throw yours away. I do, however, believe you can actively balance outside influences with personal one-on-one experiences that nurture, prepare, and guide your daughter in the pursuit and discovery of her authentic identity.

For centuries, we have been made aware that adolescence marks the beginning of the most complex and radical transition girls will experience. Parents, educators, and the general population should not be surprised by the behavioral shifts that predominate these years. Mead suggested that instead, parents and the culture should be prepared to guide, support, and stabilize the emerging identities of this population. Mead believed that if families and the culture did this, girls would experience less anxiety, confusion, and emotional or psychological distress during this transitional period.

No parents could have been in greater need of this counsel than Heather's. After Heather tried to end her life by taking pills, her parents struggled to find the strength to become such pillars of wisdom and support that Mead called for. In my office, they questioned themselves, voiced guilt and shame for not having seen the tragedy coming, and battled hopelessness. Thriving was unimaginable; "just getting through it" was all they hoped for.

Heather's parents were also angry and scrambling to blame anyone they could hold responsible. It was not until they were willing to look at their own lives that they began to understand how a long history of unhealthy relationships in their family had brought them to that awful day. For the first time in years, Heather's parents paused long enough to see clearly what had become reality for Heather. From this new perspective, they were able to stop labeling her withdrawal and oppositional behavior as "normal" for girls that age. This opened the door to an incredible opportunity to transform patterns of behavior that had almost brought death to their family.

By the time she was twelve, Heather had grown weary of trying to matter to anyone, especially to her parents. She had taken on the role of protector and pleaser in her family since early childhood. Her parents argued often and threatened divorce, leaving insecurity and fear in Heather's path. Heather soothed her two younger sisters, projecting a circle of safety when she herself felt alone and confused. Heather became the "good, responsible child" who didn't have any problems or needs—the child easiest to overlook.

As she entered middle school, Heather gradually extended her caretaker role to her peers, whom she longed to befriend. On Facebook, her nickname was "Helpful Heather." Her profile showed a smiling girl with more than 400 virtual friends, none of whom guessed the girl who always made them feel better was desperately lonely and wanted to end her life.

Late at night when she should have been sleeping, Heather watched videos of her favorite female music artists, imagining how easy life would be if only she were as pretty, powerful, and popular as they were. When she wasn't virtually connected, she felt alone. Heather had created an illusion while plugged into cyberspace that made her feel desired, wanted, and important. But when the lights went out and Facebook, chat rooms, and texting were unplugged, Heather was alone.

Eventually, Heather entered a sexual relationship she was not ready for and started cutting as a means to release her pain. Cutting, she would later confess, "felt good, almost like a good friend I could count on to help release the stress and help me feel better. I used to think I could never give it up, nor would I want to. But after a while, cutting didn't seem to give me the same release as before."

Heather's real world finally became too much for her to deal with. On the eve of her thirteenth birthday, Heather pulled the Tylenol PM from its hiding place, downed all the pills, crawled into bed, and fell into a restful sleep.

Fortunately, the pills did not succeed. After being discharged from the hospital, Heather and her parents began a journey to heal and redefine their relationship. Heather's desire to end her life was eventually replaced by a more honest longing to reconnect and repair her relationship with her family. After much work and growth, Heather's parents met this invitation by radically transforming how they parented their daughter.

Sitting in my office, Heather confessed to her parents for the first time what had happened: "When I took those pills, it felt like I didn't have to pretend anymore. I didn't have to keep trying to matter or make everything right. Things just got too complicated, and, to be honest, letting go actually felt OK. I think I was ready to die."

Rather than allowing their daughter's words to paralyze them, Heather's parents learned to stay calm and present even when her truth was hard for them to hear. They learned how to listen, to validate, and to guide her through her fears rather than minimize or dismiss them as typical preteen behavior. They reestablished family traditions and activities, developing meaningful connections that had long ago been severed. By choosing to support Heather as she worked through her feelings, the family strengthened her foundation, giving her more confidence to navigate the inevitable tensions she would face in the outside world.

Heather's story is like that of many adolescent females. She did not think her parents, siblings, or peers understood how she felt or who she was. They were far too busy with their own lives to understand hers and far too quick to blame her behavior on social influences or typical pre-adolescent behavior.

Over the course of the following year, Heather's parents learned they should have never allowed "normal" to be defined by those around them. Buying into what they had heard was the norm for a preteen daughter had seduced them into accepting behaviors that blocked intimacy, understanding, and meaningful connections.

They learned that, yes, their daughter's teen years would bring emotional reactions from out of nowhere and, on occasion, look as if she had gone over to the dark side. And yes, her persistent push for independence might feel like Darth Vader breathing down their necks, but they now understood that their work was to stay present and to engage with these tensions, not avoid them. Texting was no longer their primary way of connecting. Weekly family meetings and conversations around the dinner table were balanced with time Heather spent alone, with her friends, or at school activities. In spite of Heather's initial resistance to these changes, she confessed to me in one session that she actually liked them. She said her parents made her feel she was important to their family.

As Heather's family found—as countless families I've met through thirty years of clinical practice have found—connecting and staying connected are the most important things you can do to help your daughter and your entire family. The rituals described in this book offer parents a creative and meaningful way to establish and maintain strong connections throughout their daughters' preteen and adolescent years. The next chapter explores how rituals accomplish this.

Chapter 3

Why Rituals?

There's no doubt that the tween and teen years can challenge even the strongest of family bonds. Though your daughter's brain, body, bullies, and boyfriends may cause havoc in family relationships, you can choose not to sit on the sidelines. Instead, I encourage parents to stabilize their daughter's transition into adolescence by implementing a series of rituals that prepare and empower her to hold on to what she values.

Rituals define a significant transitional point, a movement toward something new in your daughter's life. During her preteen years, she is moving toward a new landscape: adolescence—a socially, emotionally, and physically unfamiliar place. Rituals build and prepare her inner world so that she can feel more self-confident and self-aware and so that she will identify with those who support her as she ventures forth to explore and orient herself in the world beyond home.

Rituals that mark this transition, or rite of passage, into young womanhood have been practiced for centuries in cultures all over the world, such as Aboriginal Initiation Ceremonies, the Apache Sunrise Ceremony, the Ghanaian Puberty Rite of Dipo, the Inuit Coming of Age ceremony, and many others. The rituals that are still practiced differ widely, but they share the common goal of helping girls connect more deeply to themselves, to their community, to their roles as adult women, and to the collective wisdom and heritage of their tribes. Parents and elders in the communities participate in the rituals and become allies who protect and nurture the girls to ensure their safe crossing.

Although designed and organized differently today, the Apache Sunrise Ceremony (or *Na'ii'ees*) and similar coming-of-age ceremonies continue to be practiced among southwestern tribes in the United States. The Sunrise Ceremony is celebrated to mark the sacred coming of age for girls. The summer after the onset of menses, girls are honored by their elders and supported by their community as they undergo four demanding days of dancing, singing, blessings, and other sacred ceremonies. Throughout the four days, a trusted elder woman who has been chosen by the girl's family acts as a godmother, offering the girl drink, encouragement, and food. Reenacting the ancient and sacred myth of the White Woman, the girl is painted with a mixture of clay and cornmeal, signifying that she has made the transition from a child into a young woman and taken on a sacred position within her tribe. By the end of the ritual, weakness, exhaustion, and self-doubt are overruled by the girl's ability to tap into and access the strength, power, and fortitude necessary to withstand and successfully move through the ordeal.

Today, many of these ancient rituals are judged as unacceptable practices that minimize young women rather than honor them. When taken out of context of the culture, that might make sense to our twenty-first-century minds. What is crucial to understand, though, is that the intention and result of these rituals in the context of the culture did just the opposite. In fact, rituals were celebrations intended to help girls identify their fears and develop the courage and awareness not to surrender to those fears, empowering them to trust their instincts and emerge with a new level of self-confidence. Today in the United States, rituals that mark a rite of passage are diluted and commercialized rather than used as the cornerstone of successfully crossing from one stage of development to the next. Far too many significant turning points in girls' lives are marked with sex, alcohol, hazing, and self-harming behaviors. The importance and impact of this sacred crossing—not only for girls but also for their families and communities—have been watered down, lost, or forgotten.

I am not suggesting that meaningful customs or traditions that mark significant events for girls are not part of life in the United States. Birthday parties, funerals, weddings, religious and holiday traditions, and significant family customs are meaningful and necessary in the lives of family and community. In my family, our children and now our grandchildren take turns lighting the star on top of the Christmas tree, signifying the birth of light and hope in our world and within each of us. Although this has become an important and anticipated tradition among our family members, as many families might celebrate, it is not a ritual.

Rituals do not negate the importance of family traditions and customs. They offer a deeper, life-changing experience that neither traditions nor customs can reach. Rituals are different than familiar social or family activities in that they are intentional experiences that have emotional, spiritual, and psychological meaning. They affirm transitions from one status in life to another, as in childhood to adulthood. Rituals provide experiences that shape a new understanding and use symbols that act as guides to connect girls to their deepest core, literally shaping their brains, encoding beliefs, and enhancing understanding and wisdom that influence, if not dictate, both present and future development of their personalities.

Is adapting rituals appropriate for a modern family? I believe so, as did mythologist and scholar Joseph Campbell. In the PBS series *The Power of Myth*, he offered insight on this very topic:

> The modern world lacks an essential characteristic—meaningful rituals and rites of passage for youth. . . . Unless adolescents, with the help of elders and guides, transcend their fears and cultivate a solid sense of their autonomy during this stage of their development, they will be held hostage to insecurities throughout their lives.[1]

The codirector of the Center for Youth Ministry Studies and Assistant Professor of Youth at North Park University and Theological Seminary in Chicago agrees. In her article "Fish Guts and Pig Intestines: Rites of Passage for Adolescent Girls," Ginny Olson writes:

> When a community doesn't have a formalized rite of passage into womanhood, girls will find a way to create their own. Peer initiation rites sometimes include girls piercing each other's ears at a slumber party, drinking a toast to a friend who loses her virginity, or getting a tattoo on their first spring break away from their family. In girl gang initiations, girls might be asked to commit a drive-by or other crime, or they're 'jumped in' (having to take a beating without retaliation) or 'sexed in' (where potential members are forced to have sex with male gang members, one or sometimes a group) in order to prove their commitment to the gang.[2]

Unfortunately, these rites of passage do mark life transitions for some girls, but they do nothing to evoke power, encourage independence, or build lasting self-confidence. If anything, they cast a negative pall over a girl's journey into and through adolescence.

The core purpose of rituals is to mark a significant life transition that stands apart from everyday life and evokes growth toward ownership of one's identity. Fear of the unknown, confusion, and transformation are typically associated with this passage. Wholesome rituals stabilize the confusion, build confidence to transcend fears, and support this passage in ways that build connections and empower creativity, resulting in a more developed, self-directed individual. Far too many of today's rituals seem empty, offering few of these qualities to young girls.

Meaningful rituals are effective and essential for countless reasons. Constructing rituals appropriate for girls today is a powerful, practical, and cost-effective way for parents to build honest and open communication and experiences that deepen understanding at a time when girls often feel abandoned or misunderstood, resulting in feeling their only source for comfort is social networking or peer groups. Healthy and meaningful communication stabilizes and deepens girls' connections with their parents and family members. It builds confidence in those relationships, empowering girls to stand rather than surrender when they encounter outside voices asking them to do everything their inner voice is screaming not to do. Well-planned, personalized rituals are intentional celebrations that build a girl's sense of self from the inside, empowering her to draw from that place when she comes up against external pressures from peers, academics, social networking, and media.

So where do you begin? Most parents who enter my office are willing to take action but unsure of what to do. This process begins with fostering a girl's developmental need for independence while also nurturing her equally strong need to stay connected. Girls do not have to abandon one to accommodate the other. When you navigate these two extremes without forcing your daughter to make a choice, the turbulence of her preteen and teenage years begins to relax. If your daughter learns early on that she can remain authentically herself in her relationships with you, she realizes she deserves to do this with others as well.

The best time to begin this change is during your daughter's preteen years, before the storm of adolescence wreaks havoc on her innocence and disrupts her opinions, values, and self-esteem. The tween years bring the most rapid and dramatic change in your daughter's development since infancy. The transition into middle school evokes all kinds of fears and self-doubt as she responds to the pressure to fit in and feel accepted. Girls often tell me that in spite of acting as if they don't want their parents involved in their lives, they actually crave it.

Ideally, the introduction of rituals should happen before all these stresses and pressures, not after. In actuality, though, parents and daughters of all ages can begin right where they are today. As in the relationship between Heather and her parents, relationships do not need to be perfect or pretty to begin. And even if your daughter is past (or way past) her preteen years, it is never too late to communicate love, encouragement, and support to her. If she is willing to participate, you can construct the rituals and experiences in this book so that they are age-appropriate and congruent to your daughter's needs. Chapter 10 addresses this topic in detail, but it is important to understand that the rituals given here are suggestions and can be changed to suit the needs of you and your family.

Part II of this book teaches you how to create your own rituals that begin providing a safe passage by which your daughter can not only survive her teenage years but thrive in them. These rituals consist of specific, meaningful, and individualized activities that help you encourage your daughter to identify her own interests, express herself her own way, and form her own values that will mold and strengthen her self-image before it is challenged by peers and social pressures. In teaching parents how to incorporate rituals in their lives, I have seen consistently that they anchor a girl's journey into adolescence. They are a powerful and healthy alternative to the negative forces girls experience. I have witnessed rituals connect preteens to their internal beauty, build confidence about their talents, provide a deeper awareness of their intelligence, and open their eyes to the love of the families that surround and protect them.

As you begin to implement the ideas in the following chapters, be patient with yourselves and with your daughter. This method results in powerful changes, but they don't happen overnight and won't come without friction. Bursts of resistance are inevitable. What matters most is how you respond to the friction. When Heather's parents made the choice to step into change and experience friction without fear, they opened themselves to strengthened connections and, yes, even joy. I encourage you to offer your daughter no less.

Without a new response, nothing will change the tumult of this time for young girls. I believe there can be a new narrative around this transition, but it demands that parents take action. Margaret Mead challenged the North American culture to reevaluate the ways in which it nurtures girls as they move through their adolescent years. She asked, "Under conditions such as a different response from their culture, could a girl's passage from childhood to young womanhood be less stressful and less traumatic?"[3] Parents and daughters who have created rituals during their daughters' preteen years overwhelmingly answer Mead's question with a resounding "Yes." The tradition of rituals that prepare and strengthen your daughter's inner identity *before* she ventures into the unknown, begins to explore new surroundings, and struggles to master independence are a concrete, powerful place to start transforming your daughter's experience as a teenager.

As you construct these rituals, consider the following results you want your daughter to experience:

- Gain a sense of power and confidence.

- Experience a deepened level of self-knowledge and self-reliance she was not aware of prior to the ritual.
- Come to know and assume her identity within her community, her family, and, most importantly, herself.
- Stabilize connections and build support within families and with parents, communities, and significant elders in her life.

PART II:
Rituals for All Ages

After thirty years of working with female adolescents and parents, I realized that parents need a hands-on, doable process to transform this period of their daughters' lives from something that parents just want to "get through" to something they can celebrate. Reviving the ancient practice of marking this life passage as important and sacred with a ritual is essential in order to strengthen family connections. I encourage parents to seize this time in their daughter's life as a golden opportunity to reinforce her desires, validate her dreams, and deepen family relationships.

This section provides parents with practical ideas for rituals to help their daughter pursue her desires, strengthen her autonomy, and trust her wisdom while empowering them to take back their role as wise elders who engage and stabilize their daughter's transition. The stages outlined in the following chapters have been adapted from the work of author and Jungian analyst James Hollis. Parents will learn to engage and guide their daughter through these years of self-discovery by marking each year from age eight through thirteen with rituals that serve a specific purpose and build on the preceding stage. Once implemented, the hands-on, step-by-step lessons in this book can successfully help parents navigate the teen years and strengthen their daughter's connection to her family, her community, and, most importantly, herself.

Chapter 4

Getting Started

The hardest part of incorporating rituals into the fabric of your family is taking that first step. It's not easy to introduce concepts that are perhaps unfamiliar to those who mean the most to you. Fear of rejection, confusion, embarrassment—these are natural at the precipice of any change, yet I encourage you to move forward one step at a time. As you read the stories that follow about real families who have adopted these meaningful rituals into their lives, you'll learn not just that it *can* be done but that you will be glad you did it—and, most importantly, so will your daughter.

So, how to really begin? It may first be helpful to understand what *not* to do. No party hats, no balloons, no gifts wrapped in bows or glittery paper. This is not to be associated with typical birthday celebrations. These mark a sacred crossing, so it is important to focus on connections and not on "stuff."

You need to choose a location where the ritual celebration will take place, preferably a room or area away from your daughter's peers, home, and other familiar influences. It is important that she recognize that this is different than her usual world. Families can choose any location to celebrate, like a campsite, a picnic area, or a room at a nearby YMCA or church. It does not have to involve a lot of money or extravagant planning, and it shouldn't be difficult. Try to create an experience in a place that will be positive for all involved, especially your daughter.

The guest list comes next. When you invite people who have played a significant role in your daughter's life, it is important to educate them regarding the meaning, purpose, and process of this celebration. It is also helpful to explain what is expected of them during the ritual. Laying the groundwork in advance gives everyone time to think through their contributions to your daughter's life and the commitment they will make in helping her grow into a secure, confident young woman. When participants understand the meaning behind the event, they show up engaged in the process.

The key is to not make the plans too complicated for yourself or those who participate. Reflect on your family and build an experience that will fit your personalities, values, and comfort levels. Most family members report that the ritual felt awkward at first but that they soon relaxed and found it meaningful. By being creative and using objects around your home, costs can be kept to a minimum and still yield meaningful results. Stir your imagination, pick a spot, and start planning. The case studies included for each ritual in the chapters that follow illustrate how actual families did just that.

Chapter 5

Ritual One: Separation

❁ Age Eight ❁

As the first step of a girl's passage into young womanhood, Separation is an essential developmental transition. For years, I have lectured and written about Separation, teaching parents about the importance of this time and helping them create rituals that would mark the beginning of this significant turning point in their relationship with their daughters.

The ritual of Separation and the final ritual, the Return, incorporate family members or close friends who have had influential roles in your daughter's life. A girl's parents or primary caretakers typically facilitate the other rituals.

The Meaning of Separation

When girls turn eight, they begin a significant developmental transition. With one foot rooted deeply in their past and one foot stretching into adolescence, they experience a gap between these two stages of development that stirs confusion, uncertainty, and chaos in them as well as their parents. At this juncture, girls need to know their roots will stay intact while they explore the life that lies beyond the secure environment they have known. Connection and communication can normalize this crossing between girlhood and young womanhood.

Separation, the first stage of preadolescence, marks the beginning of many changes that will redefine the relationship between parent and child. This step in a girl's life represents the beginning of her physical and emotional movement away from her parents and her greater connection with those outside her family. Soon she will want to hang out with peers more than parents and talk to friends for hours while offering little information to her family when asked about her day. This shift in her can feel sudden and abrupt when, in reality, her movement toward independence has been gestating since birth.

From the moment children are born, their biological need for separation, beginning with the severing of the umbilical cord, enables them to survive. In girls' early years, parents may have thought their gestures of independence were cute, endearing, or even funny. However, eight, nine, and ten years later, parents begin to wonder what happened to those cherished moments when the very same biological need for separation shows up as rolling eyes, slamming doors, and spending the evening in their rooms rather than spending time with their families. Although not as pretty or as easily understood, these behaviors are as developmentally important as the ones parents once found entertaining.

Throughout history, myths and fairy tales have told stories of girls being lured away from their families and into the woods by an animal. When the youth enters the forest, the animal turns into a helpful guide. While the girl searches for what she needs to survive on her own, the wise guide offers support and encourages the girl to trust her own wisdom. In these myths and fairy tales, as in real life, this journey and separation from what she has always known—with the help of the wise guide—is essential for her transformation. Without it, the girl lives in an unhealthy, fearful, dependent manner.

Frank Baum's enduring tale *The Wonderful Wizard of Oz* provides a vivid example of this. Dorothy no longer finds understanding and meaning at home. Fearful and confused, she thinks she must leave home to get someone to take her seriously, so she enters the outside world in search of someone who will listen and understand her. By doing this, Dorothy takes her first step out of childhood—a dependent state—and embarks on a journey to the discovery of her wisdom, love for herself, and courage—all that she needs to become more independent and face the challenges of her young adult world.

In her article "*The Wizard of Oz* and the Path to Enlightenment," Jeanne M. House states, "Unlike the fairy tales of its day, [author Frank Baum's] child heroine was not a meek and mild victim but [a young girl] who transforms from a dependent people-pleaser to one who gains an indomitable spirit and courageous attitude, while pioneering new trails in order to find Home,"[1] which, in Baum's story as in dream analysis, represents one's Self. This transformation could not have happened if Dorothy had stayed in Kansas. Joseph Campbell argued that young people must go to an unfamiliar landscape to accomplish the separation necessary to successfully move into young adulthood.[2] This need is no different for the twenty-first-century girl than it was for Dorothy in the early 1900s.

During a girl's preadolescent years, when the rumblings of adolescence stir, I encourage parents to create conversations, connections, and celebrations that help their daughter understand the confusion she experiences that may make her act out. Rather than resist a daughter's natural movement from dependence to independence, parents can look underneath her reactions and guide the exploration of emotions that are dictating irrational behaviors. This insight teaches her to think about and process the conflict she is experiencing, understand it, and react in ways that work for her rather than against her. Taking the time to help her bridge this turbulent gap teaches her to internally pause and move through her emotions rather than remain confused by them.

Supporting change and independence while being fearful of it can feel like walking a tightrope for parents. Separation is the opportunity for you to choose to join your daughter's journey, rather than disconnect from it, by marking the first step of her movement into young adulthood. Preparing your daughter for what lies ahead rather than waiting until she is deep in the chaos of adolescence relaxes the confusion she will experience.

Ritual One: Separation

This ritual affirms the beginning stage of your daughter's passage into adolescence by surrounding her with a circle of support. These special people should be family or close friends who represent the strength, self-compassion, and wisdom she will need to gain in order to own her independence. This provides her a safe landing pad where she can return whenever she feels confused or in need of reassurance or guidance. This ritual paves the way for girls to discover their identity rather than derive it from others.

As the following stories illustrate, there are a number of ways to facilitate the Separation ritual. Though three different rituals are described, all of them include family and close friends coming together and bearing symbols of strength, compassion, and support for the young girl.

Emmy's Story: A First Step

When my oldest granddaughter, Emmy, turned eight, I wanted her and her parents to experience what I had been teaching others in my clinical practice. Witnessing our family put this ritual into action deepened my belief in the necessity and relevance of empowerment rituals and what they offer to a girl's developmental process.

At eight, the drama of Emmy's preteen life had just begun. Reflecting on the changes that were beginning to surface made me smile, but while I was prepared for this new side of Emmy because of my work, her bewildered parents were not. What I wanted to help Emmy and her parents understand was that underneath the spikes of discontent and soft rebellion, a creative, passionate, opinionated young woman was unfolding.

The territory that stood before Emmy would be unfamiliar and often unkind, and I wanted to make sure she had the internal resources to draw on when she arrived there. To accomplish this, I suggested that our family create a celebration that would honor who Emmy was and support the young woman she was becoming. Much of what she had learned would go with her into adolescence, and parts of her childlike personality would be left behind. I knew from working with other girls that if Emmy did not have a solid internal framework to support her as she faced the storms this stage of development would inevitably bring, she—like many girls facing preadolescence—would struggle through this season rather than thrive. The values that would come from the ritual would form cornerstones to support her journey in becoming an independent, confident, and caring young woman.

It has been almost five years since our family marked Emmy's eighth birthday. On several occasions since then, Emmy has told me that the treasure box I gave her to store the gifts given to her by her family during the ritual helped her to remember that occasion.

She said that rereading the messages family members wrote to her always helped her feel closer to her family when we weren't together or when she was feeling alone.

Recently, her grandfather and I were visiting, and Emmy called from upstairs, asking us to come up to her room because she had something to show us. When we entered, we saw her treasure box open and all of the gifts from her first ritual displayed on her desk. She showed us each one, recounting her memory of the gift and who gave it to her. Holding up a red heart, Emmy asked, "Remember this, Granddy? You told me that when you were young, you had a hard time following your heart. You wanted me to always remember to trust mine. And remember this one, the play cell phone that Aunt Shannon gave me? Kind of weird now, 'cause I have my own cell phone. Aunt Shannon told me that there would be times when I would feel like I couldn't talk with Mom or Dad about stuff and that she would be there to listen if I needed someone else to talk with. I never thought that would happen, but she knew what she was talking about, because sometimes my parents just don't get it. And do you remember this one?" she asked, pointing to a picture of her Uncle Phillip holding her at the beach. "He would always put me on his shoulders when we were in the water. At the ritual, he told me to always know that he would be around to lean on whenever I needed him. I don't see him much, but I really think he would do that if I asked."

Emmy then pulled out the only gift left in her box. "This one," she said, holding it up, "is my favorite." Her cousin Halee, who was also eight, even then the aspiring actress in our family, had walked over to Emmy during the ritual and presented a small container of Play-Doh. Turning to the group, Halee vividly explained that she and Emmy had always had fun playing together. She described in humorous detail the stunts they had pulled, jokes they had played on parents, and crazy food mixtures they had made to trick Emmy's younger sister into eating them. The mood of the ritual shifted from serious to hysterical as those two young girls exchanged laughter and stories, deepening a connection that seemed to surprise even them.

Then Halee quietly turned to Emmy and told her that she would always be there to make her laugh if she was sad and to laugh with her when she was happy. "Whenever you need a friend to play with or just be with, I'm always here, Emmy. I love you, and I don't want you to forget that—even when we get all big and grown up."

When Halee spoke the last few words, Emmy's eyes filled with tears. Each of us experienced our connection as a family—and, most importantly, our connection to Emmy—deepen in ways we had never experienced together before.

Closing her treasure box, now also filled with memories from two other rituals, Emmy returned it to the bottom shelf of her bookcase. She turned to us with a huge smile on her face and said softly, "Grammy and Granddy, this is the best gift I have ever been given. I don't think I will ever grow too old for this."

Mary's Story: Quilt of Courage

Mary's family decided to rent a cabin in the mountains to celebrate their daughter's entry into preadolescence. Because she had no siblings, her grandparents were deceased, and other relatives lived far away, Mary's parents invited a childhood friend and close adult friends whom their daughter knew well, including Mary's youth pastor, her Girl Scout leader, and an elderly woman who had taken care of Mary during her early childhood.

Mary had recently learned to quilt, so her parents asked each participant to bring a square of fabric with a design that represented their relationship to Mary or their wish for her. The intention was that Mary and her mother would sew the squares into a small quilt as a reminder of each participant's connection to and support of Mary. Mary had been told about the ritual, but not who would be there or what would occur.

When Mary entered the room, she was surprised to see people she had not expected in the unfamiliar setting, and she felt awkward at first. Her parents served hot chocolate and cookies to give Mary a chance to connect with everyone in the gathering, then they invited everyone to join them at a campfire behind the cabin. They had placed blankets in a circle around the fire. When everyone was seated, Mary's parents began the ceremony by explaining the purpose of the gathering and thanking everyone for coming. After singing a few songs, the participants took turns giving Mary their pieces of fabric, explaining their significance for them and for Mary.

Mary's scout leader had embroidered a badge of courage onto the piece of material she gave to Mary. Handing it to Mary, she said, "Mary, I recall when you first entered our troop. You were shy, you stayed by yourself, and you seemed afraid to speak up. Within a short time, you began to take part and even took on a leadership role, and you served your troop well. As you stepped out, your troop was able to experience the courage and creative mind you had kept inside. This symbol of courage, the lion, is to remind you to not be fearful of letting others see the wonderful, smart, and powerful young lady you are."

Following her words, others began sharing what they had brought, which led to a couple of hours of storytelling. This relaxed the mood and brought laughter and conversation to the circle.

When there were no more words, the ritual closed with everyone roasting marshmallows, drinking hot cider, and sitting around the fire until the embers signaled the evening's end.

When everyone left, Mary, her parents, and her childhood friend spent the remainder of the weekend in the mountains. They played games, went on hikes, and sewed Mary's quilt, which she later decided to call her Quilt of Courage.

Several months after her weekend away, Mary walked into my office and dropped her backpack at my feet. She plopped down in a nearby chair and spoke with a sense of clarity and confidence I had not experienced during the year we had worked together.

"Well, aren't you going to ask me what's in my backpack?"

Engaging her playful spirit, I asked, "Do you want me to?"

A smile began to take over her face as she moved out of her chair and gently began pulling the quilt out of her backpack, spreading it over the space between us. "Dr. Maria, we have talked a lot about knowing who I am and exploring things I like or what I'm interested in. Well, this is who I am. This is my identity for now. The quilt's not finished, and I'm not either. But for now, I'm just as beautiful as this quilt, and a lot of people have helped make me beautiful, just like they did this quilt. So, I think I'm good for now. But before we finish here, I wanted you to see one of the best birthday gifts that I have ever gotten, my Quilt of Courage. I'm going to hang it in my room to remind me of all the great parts of myself and all the people who believe in me."

As Mary spoke, it was too difficult to hold back tears of pure joy and celebration. Deciding I had no need to hide them, I let them come, as did she. Mary and I sat in silence a few moments, knowing that her work, for now, was truly finished. Mary had come a long way from the insecure, voiceless girl her parents brought into my office over a year ago. To mark our final session and the beginning of Mary's discovery and ownership of Self, I asked her to explain each piece of fabric on her quilt, which she was delighted to do in detail.

When Mary left, I was aware of the profound importance rituals can play in helping girls tap into their inherent power and in deepening connections to people who will support and encourage them as they begin their passage toward young womanhood.

Anna's Story: A Table of Memories

When Anna turned eight, her parents marked the beginning stage of her passage into young adulthood with a ceremony that would be different than the birthday celebrations she had experienced in the past. Several months prior to the celebration, her parents invited family members and a few close friends to the ritual, asking them to bring an object that would symbolize their connection to Anna. Each participant was invited to think about the significance of the item they would bring and were asked to explain how it represented what they wished for Anna as she grew into this new time in her life.

Wanting to be creative and keep expenses down, Anna's parents chose objects their family had collected or crafted during the past eight years, including drawings, report cards, pictures, poetry, a piano piece Anna had performed in a recital, a small remnant of her baby blanket, ballet slippers, and a baseball glove. The childhood memorabilia wove a story that visually portrayed significant moments from Anna's eight years.

After the guests gathered and spent time becoming acquainted, Anna's parents asked everyone to find a seat around the picnic table. Going around the table, each person shared a story about an object on the table that had meaning for them before adding the gift they had brought, explaining its significance and what they wished for Anna as she grew into this new phase of her life.

Finally, Anna's oldest brother, Mark, took his turn. Picking up a small, frayed piece of baby blanket and replacing it with a new stadium blanket he had bought at his freshman orientation, he turned to his little sister. For a few moments, this six-foot-tall, burly brother struggled for words. Gaining his composure, he began to speak.

"Anna, I remember when Mom brought you home from the hospital all wrapped up in that pink baby blanket, and I remember you taking that dumb thing around everywhere you went. For some reason, you thought it would protect you. You embarrassed me back then, but I get it now." Picking up the stadium blanket, Mark leaned over to his sister and handed it to her. "Anna, I always want you to feel safe and protected. But it's OK to be afraid—I get that way sometimes. I may not be here to take care of you and protect you from all the crazy stuff that can happen as you get into middle school and high school, but I want to give you a new blanket to wrap up in and even carry around if you want to—kind of like a reminder that even when I'm away at college, you can count on me if you ever need to." Mark closed out the ritual with his gift to Anna. Afterward, all participants were invited to enjoy homemade ice cream, Anna's favorite dessert.

Three years after that celebration, I had the opportunity to ask Anna what she remembered about it. Without hesitation, she said, "My brother's promise. He never forgot that. My first year in middle school was horrible at first; I started out with no friends and really felt like a loser. I would text Mark and let him know how crummy I felt, and he always found time to call or text back. He would remind me of all the things I was good at, all the things he liked about me. Sometimes I just needed that."

Rituals connect families in ways they would have never imagined. They facilitate experiences that allow family members to tap into a deeper part of themselves and create memories that stay long after the event is over. They do not replace gifts or celebrations; they deepen them. Creating meaningful rituals that speak to your daughter's inner world prepares and empowers her to enter the world that awaits her.

Daughters will separate from their parents, and a parent's greatest work is to prepare them so they can. Neither Mary, Anna, nor

Emmy will do their journey perfectly. In spite of the good efforts of their parents, there will be scars, tears, despair, and rebellion. Rituals do not protect girls or families from that; what they do is prepare them to successfully navigate through them, starting with Separation and then moving beyond.

Chapter 6

Ritual Two: Letting Go

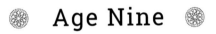 **Age Nine**

The nature of life demands change. Throughout early child-hood, girls are physically dependent on their families and psychologically identify themselves in relation to their family unit. Within this landscape, they fit in and feel that they belong. As girls mature and enter a new cycle of development, however, their landscape shifts. They begin to explore who they are in relation to the roles that have identified them within the family, and they question their place in it. The lens through which girls see themselves begins to refract the light in new ways, offering a new perspective for seeing themselves in relationship to their families. "I" becomes distinct from "we." While girls continue to care about and notice how they fit into their parents' lives, they also begin to see themselves as a separate entity, as an individual within their family.

The Meaning of Letting Go

At approximately age nine, your daughter enters her adolescent preseason, during which her independence and self-knowledge continue to evolve. Her brain releases a surge of creative energy that awakens curiosity about her body, her thoughts, her beliefs, and her interests. These changes activate a desire to be involved in decision-making about family schedules and activities; she wants to negotiate her role in family dynamics. She continues to need the approval, guidance, and support of her parents, but she is experiencing the natural, healthy development of her capacity to be more responsible and involved in family interactions.

As she stands on the cusp of her tween years, your daughter is ready to re-explore, redefine, and reorient her identity in your family. She begins to let go of what no longer serves her and explore what does. Her attitudes change. As her parents, you will notice behaviors and interests that have been around since her childhood begin to disappear. Some days, she will cling to them like a thin, worn blankie, and then, without warning, she will find them embarrassingly childish.

The Letting Go ritual coincides with these biological and emotional drives. The ritual normalizes and affirms her developing interest in the world outside of what she knows while stabilizing her need to remain connected to her family. It paves the way for your daughter to discover her identity rather than derive it from others. In your efforts to encourage her exploration, you need not surrender your authority or wisdom. In his book *Brainstorm: The Power of the Teenage Brain*, Daniel Siegel suggests that parents can "provide a safe haven while also encouraging exploration." Siegel asks the question that most parents ask: "How do we find a balance between our adolescent's personal decisions and our parental regulation, our concern?" He writes that he and his wife found their answer:

> Structure with empowerment is how my wife and I would think of our strategy of parenting. How could we support our adolescents while also allowing them to find their own voices? And how at the same time could we set the limits and cautions our own years of living had taught us? Science would call this 'authoritative parenting,' a helpful approach that is filled with warmth, limit setting, and honoring of autonomy in age-appropriate ways. Such a stance is also the balanced approach of secure attachment: lending support while supporting separation.[1]

When parents create an environment that fosters safety while nurturing growth, girls are more likely to develop the personal strength needed to risk exploring who they are separate from their past. The Letting Go ritual offers this stability.

Ritual Two: Letting Go

This ritual provides your daughter the opportunity to explore what aspects of her younger self no longer fit and encourages her to engage new, creative aspects of her personality. By offering her guided experiences that support her need for more freedom, you aid her development into a self-confident and self-aware teen.

The ritual encourages her to trust her desire to explore her own thoughts, to make decisions, to participate in defining her role in the family, and to try out new ideas. Through the ritual, she learns that this is normal and healthy and that you support her in this process.

The Process

Step 1: Start the Conversation

Tell your daughter that as part of celebrating her ninth year, you would like to talk about changes in how she experiences herself at age nine compared to a year ago. You can explain that at around her age, girls usually want more freedom and responsibility in making decisions that involve them. You also might want to share a few observations of changes you've noticed in her behaviors and needs.

Step 2: Make Time to Connect

Suggest that you and she choose a time and private place where she can share those changes with you as well as her thoughts about what she would like to change, let go of, or add in her life, including the way she is treated at home. You may need to assure her that she can be totally honest about what she wants and doesn't want. This is critical in helping you support and guide her to become less dependent on you and more self-reliant. This open sharing isn't easy for many girls and may require several conversations until you both are comfortable talking about this topic openly.

Step 3: Document Her Ideas

Explain that you or she will write down what she wants to let go of and her new needs and desires; these will become the basis for her individualized ritual. The way her ideas are recorded can take several forms. For example, I suggested that one set of parents ask their daughter to collect rocks and write on each a behavior, belief, or role in her family that she no longer wanted to identify with. After she wrote on the rocks, they put them in a backpack, which she put on. They discussed what it had been like for her to carry these thoughts, beliefs, and roles around throughout her childhood and now, at the age of nine, how it felt to continue carrying them around. If you use this way of writing her thoughts, you can then help your daughter explore what it might feel like to take them out of her backpack and no longer carry them around. Then you can ask your daughter what she would like to do with each rock. I've seen girls choose a number of options, including putting them in the garden, putting them in a special box kept under her bed, or throwing each rock, one at a time, into a nearby river, ocean, or lake. However your daughter chooses to release the rocks, suggest that each one be a reminder of how she is changing and how it feels to let these roles, feelings, and beliefs go.

This is just one example. There are many different ways to help your daughter enact this ritual. In the story that follows, I suggested to Lily's parents another path that allowed their daughter to explore, communicate, and reorient herself within their family system.

Lily's Story: Opening Up

Lily, a nine-year-old soon-to-be fourth grader, had been diagnosed with diabetes before she was two years old. For years, she and her parents had radically adjusted their lives to save hers. Wakeful nights, panicked trips to the ER, threatening infections, and sugar levels that forced Lily to be pulled from class and rushed to the nurse's office were part of Lily's everyday life. An insulin pump, a glucose monitor, and a clunky wristwatch that checked her sugar levels were unwanted accessories to her daily wardrobe.

Lily's parents had noticed she showed less patience and more resistance in her interactions with her younger brother and in her participation in family activities. Adding to their concern, they learned from her dentist that Lily had begun grinding her teeth in her sleep. These were sharp changes from the accommodating, compliant, seemingly happy girl who had taken her life in stride up until recently.

With her parents' encouragement, Lily spoke openly about what she was feeling. She described how stressed she was about starting the fourth grade. Then she confessed that she felt her parents treated her like a baby. Having her dad check on her sugar levels throughout the school day and when she was at home annoyed her. The more they let her talk, the more Lily opened up about the routine of her care and the vigilant control of her health and safety that she felt her parents had.

She was especially angry and frustrated that she had to be connected to her parents through her diabetes smart watch, made by Pebble, even when she was at a friend's house.

"I can't do anything wrong or you get worried that I'll die! I don't want to go to the fourth grade and have my friends look at me every time the Pebble vibrates with a message from Dad telling me my levels are down and that I need to eat a snack. When that happens, kids ask all kinds of questions. Besides, it's big and looks weird. I hate it, and I'm tired of wearing it."

The following day, Lily's mother, familiar with my work with rituals for preteens, called and asked my advice. I suggested that they invite Lily to participate in the Letting Go ritual, and they agreed. Afterward, Lily's mother described their experience:

"After Lily unloaded to us what she had held in for months, she was able to move past her anger and anxiety and explore ideas about what we could fix. Her eyes lit up when I suggested the Letting Go ritual. Lily loved the idea as soon as we explained its meaning and purpose. She needed no prompting.

"Lily decided to write down on different-colored Post-it notes behaviors she wanted to let go of. She asked us to wait outside her bedroom until she was ready to show us the Post-it notes. About fifteen minutes later, she called us in. The first Post-it note I saw on her wall had *Perfectionism!* written in bright red. Seven other Post-it notes expressed different behaviors she wanted to let go of, including *Not having to go to bed at the same time as my brother, Getting to close my door when I'm in my room with my friends, Not wearing the Pebble to school,* and *Dad not calling.* (Lily later amended this by saying, 'Dad, you can just call their mom and she can tell you if I'm OK, or you can text my Pebble and I'll text you back. Just don't call!')

"The three of us discussed each note and explored how we could work together. We started by focusing on the three that were most important to her: perfectionism, wearing the Pebble watch, and Dad not calling. At the end of our conversation, I asked Lily what she wanted to do with her Letting Go notes. She wasn't sure, so I suggested we burn them. She could let the fire symbolize the energy, power, intuition, and wisdom that were part of the new self she was discovering. Lily thought that was a great idea.

"The next day, we put the notes under a rock in a fireproof container outdoors. Before burning each note, Lily closed her eyes and said out loud what she wanted to let go of. She said, 'Perfectionism—I don't want to feel I have to be perfect any longer, for anybody.' As the note burned, we closed our eyes and imagined the smoke letting perfectionism go and rise to the sky. She proceeded to burn the other two notes as well. Closing the ritual, Lily's father leaned over to her and said: 'I'm proud that you let go of trying to be different than who you are.' Lily smiled with a joy we had not seen in weeks. For the moment, her anxiety and stress seemed to have lifted with the smoke."

Toward the end of the school year, Lily's mother brought me up to date. "Throughout Lily's ninth year, we repeated the ritual as needed. More 'Letting Go' notes followed: letting go of blaming herself when her little brother tried to run away from home after they fought; letting go of feeling like she always had to say yes. The Letting Go ritual has become part of our family life as a tool for teaching Lily to be aware of sources of stress and share them with us and also to create ways of relief from them. Sometimes just writing the words on the notes and posting them on her wall helps her to let go of specific worries.

"Then, not long ago, Lily told us she wanted to write Post-it notes naming what she *wants*, not just what she doesn't want. We agreed but cautioned that there might be things she wants that would not be possible. Lily understood, so we created a Wanting Ritual.

"Lily wrote cards naming specific desires. She added magnets to the backs and put them on the refrigerator door for us all to see and discuss. Among her 'Want' cards have been *Take a walk in the woods, Bake and decorate something, Yoga with Mom*, and *Mom and Dad off electronics*. One card in particular caught our attention. On it was written *Just be a normal kid.*

"I asked Lily what that meant to her. As I feared, we were back to her hatred of having diabetes and everything that goes with it. I asked, 'What is the worst part about the diabetes?' To our surprise, she said, 'This watch! I told you that a long time ago. I know I have to wear it, but it makes me feel so not normal when I'm with my friends. I'm used to having diabetes, but it's this watch that I hate.'

"I had assumed Lily didn't want to wear the watch, but after giving her a chance to talk through her feelings, she proved me wrong. It was just the design that was the problem, not the fact that she had to wear it, and that opened possibilities for a solution. I had recently heard about a newer version with a better design and a more comfortable fit. Lily was thrilled. Again, talking through her wants made us aware of a need we had misunderstood. It was the watch, not the diabetes, that troubled Lily. We could easily make a huge improvement in her life with diabetes."

In many ways, this season of your daughter's life is like nature itself. Just as nature often has to shed growth to flourish, your daughter must be allowed and encouraged to do the same. My experience with parents and tweens has convinced me that working with nature is far more life-giving and enjoyable than fighting against it. In doing so, parents stabilize their daughter's life and strengthen her sense of herself in the world while staying connected as she journeys into adolescence.

Chapter 7

Ritual Three: Making Wise Connections

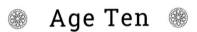 **Age Ten**

Parents or primary caregivers are the most influential people in the early years of a girl's life. If a girl develops a sense of self that is valued and understood, there is a greater chance of her moving through adolescence with stability and confidence.

At the age of ten, your daughter has completed her first decade of life. She is passing through one of the many developmental cycles in her life's journey. In the second ritual, Letting Go, your daughter learned to explore her voice, collaborate in making decisions, and envision herself within her family unit.

As her second decade begins, her interests are shifting to the unfamiliar territories of peers and new social groups. In her search for acceptance, she will try on many different roles and identities in this new landscape. Just as her growth used to be dependent on attaching and defining her place within her family system, the continued development of her autonomy requires that she now find out where she fits outside her home.

The Meaning of Making Wise Connections

At ten, girls are preparing to leave elementary school and step into the new experience of middle school. This is not an easy or smooth transition, and the territory is not as kind or nurturing as the one you provided your daughter. She will be bombarded with outside influences that are not affirming or ego building. Her peers are as confused as your daughter, and together they are impressionable youths swirling in an environment where it is easy to compromise or even lose one's self.

When the girls I work with describe their experience at this time, I hear "it's drama filled," "it's horrible," "I couldn't wait until I got out," "the worst years of my life," "I never felt I could just be myself," and "I was scared most of the time."

These years do not have to be this difficult, and this belief is shared by many of the child development experts I mention throughout this book. Your daughter's tween years present many opportunities for you to set the stage for adolescence. Before your daughter arrives at this significant transition, it is crucial that you make sure she has assistance outside her peer groups to prepare and strengthen her ego. Building on the foundation laid in Rituals

One and Two, Making Wise Connections offers creative ways to help your daughter remain connected to her inner knowledge while engaging with wise mentors to help her further define her place in the world.

The ancient proverb "It takes a village to raise a child" is often used to emphasize the significant role families and communities play in forming a child's identity, sense of self, and emotional and physical security. At this age particularly, girls need relationships outside their families that they can turn to for wisdom and instruction in making decisions that empower rather than diminish their self-esteem.

According to Mary Pipher, author "Carol Bly coined the term 'cultural abuse' for those elements in a culture that block growth and development."[1] Without a doubt, girls today are bombarded by conflicting and, at times, harmful messages and images that entice them into abusive norms that strip away their sense of self. The impact that a caring community and family play on a child's development is more important than ever. When these pillars of support are put into place, girls have options, making them less likely to surrender to risky, fleeting, and treacherous impulses.

In the 1939 film version of Baum's *The Wizard of Oz*, Glinda the Good Witch appeared to Dorothy to offer guidance and discernment, giving her the ruby slippers and directions to the Emerald City, helping her find her way. At the end of the film, Glinda told Dorothy that she had what she needed to get home all along, and having learned to confront her fears and the bullies in her life, she was ready to return home as her more developed self. Dorothy's relationship with Glinda strengthened her ability to rely on herself and her intuition when making the choices that would take her where she wanted to go in life.

In his book *The Middle Passage: From Misery to Meaning in Midlife*, James Hollis writes, "[O]ur culture has lost the mythic road map which helps locate a person in a larger context. Without a tribal vision of the gods, and their spiritual network, modern individuals are cut adrift to wander without guidance, without models and without assistance through the various life stages."[2]

During their preteen years, girls become more interested in connecting to and taking advice from outside role models such as coaches, teachers, and youth directors than their parents. They need role models who help them stay in touch with their true selves as they expand their social circles and try out ways to fit in. Wise and caring elders can help them regulate the tensions that independence and codependence create. This is an ideal time to introduce your daughter to resources and mentors who can teach her skills that support her growth.

These role models and elders are especially important because the drastic increase in time youth and adults spend with technology—TV, Internet, iPhones, chat rooms, texting, and sexting—has severely changed the landscape of interpersonal relationships, weakening adolescents' connection to and communication with parents. In fact, a large majority of behavioral and social scientists would agree that not only have social media and social networking changed the lives of families and close, interpersonal relationships, they have ruptured the developmental process of becoming an independent and whole Self.

The connections offered by wise mentors mark the third stage of a girl's passage into adolescence. Introducing your daughter to special people who offer meaningful experiences that strengthen her inner framework has a direct, positive impact on the rest of her life. Connecting your daughter to resources who can teach her valuable lessons and strategies about self-care is a way to guide her toward wise and supportive mentors that extend beyond you and her peers before her teen years even begin.

Ritual Three: Making Wise Connections

This ritual provides opportunities to connect your daughter to significant role models outside of her family. To facilitate this, the ritual introduces wise mentors to give her the opportunity to tap into her dreams and interests, trusting her power and ability to pursue them.

Such role models can guide your daughter as she navigates the turbulence these years will stir; they serve as mentors your daughter can learn from who will encourage her potential and bolster her self-worth. Building these connections now, rather than later, enhances your daughter's self-knowledge and teaches her how to explore alternative ways to process, think through, and make decisions regarding how she wants to form her identity.

If your family already has relationships with special people outside the family, consider engaging with them in a new way through your daughter's ritual. Yet another way to facilitate this ritual is to thoughtfully consider where your daughter has a need. Perhaps she is struggling with healthy choices, as in Casey's story later in this chapter. Perhaps she needs perspective on what others are going through, as happened for Sarah. There are countless opportunities to bring meaningful relationships into your daughter's life to help her grow in her understanding of her place in her world.

Wise Connection One: Listening to Dreams

Working with images and storylines from dreams, dreamers of all ages—and particularly girls at this age—can set aside preconceptions and see their relationships, concerns, and life situations with fresh eyes. Connecting with professionals who work in this field can facilitate a safe avenue for conversations about dreams, allowing girls to gain access to their own inner wisdom and become curious about what is revealed.

Emmy and Halee's Story: Inside Dreams

When Emmy and Halee celebrated their tenth birthdays, I wanted to put together a Making Wise Connections ritual for them. As I considered a ritual to connect them to external resources, I thought of Joan, a psychotherapist specializing in dream analysis who has been personally and professionally invested in helping girls develop a curiosity about their dreams.

I first asked Emmy and Halee if they would be interested in going to see a friend who helps girls understand their dreams. They agreed hesitantly, so I called my friend and scheduled a time for them to meet.

At their request, my husband and I were with them while Joan taught them about dreams. After introductions and time spent getting to know one another, the girls were discussing fears over grades, insecurities about not being athletic, shyness at their first school social, and concerns about not having friends at school. Once the door was opened to exploring their dream world, the girls were hooked and wanted to understand more about how their dreams worked.

Joan asked the girls if they remembered dreaming and whether they were curious about what their dreams might mean. As the girls relaxed, they spoke openly about dreams they'd had had in recent months. One shared a dream that had repeated throughout the year. Joan taught them how to think about possible meanings of their dreams, asking them to recall any concerns, fears, or changes happening in their lives around the times of their dreams. She taught them to pay attention to and trust their own observations and responses to the dreams rather than the opinions of friends or parents.

Afterward, Joan led the girls to a table on which she had put piles of magazines, markers of all colors, scissors, glue, and blank pieces of white cardboard. She told them to write down what they each thought was the message of their dreams. Then she instructed them to cut out pictures from the magazines that reflected the message and to make a collage they would take home. Their collage would be a symbol that marked and also reminded them of this ritual.

On the way home, Halee said, "You know, that was cool. I thought talking about dreams was going to be weird and boring. I never knew that my brain could actually talk to me when I'm sleeping. That's awesome!"

Wise Connection Two: Volunteerism

Volunteerism is a form of connection that helps girls build and strengthen positive self-esteem. Despite being biologically wired to be self-absorbed, girls at this age are open and ripe to serving others and developing empathy. When they experience volunteer work, they tend to root their self-esteem and pride in their accomplishments, contributions, and connections to their communities and home. Self-satisfaction and self-worth are born out of the awareness that they have the power to make significant changes in their world, which leads to more confidence in facing it.

At this age, girls' primary means of connecting and communicating is by electronic devices rather than face-to-face interactions. Their ability to form intimate, honest interpersonal relationships weakens, which in turn challenges their ability to develop important social skills like empathy, patience, trust, and compassion. Most importantly to this age group, their willingness to speak up and say what they feel and need weakens. Volunteerism provides hands-on opportunities for girls to practice and develop these essential skills.

Sarah's Story: On a Mission

At the end of a ten-week process group with ten-year-old girls several years ago, one of the group members asked, "Now that we have learned how to like ourselves and believe in ourselves, how can we help our friends or other people we care about learn they are important, too?"

"Good question," I said. "How would you imagine doing that?"

A burst of conversation followed about concern over friends who were involved with dangerous and self-destructive behaviors. These girls wanted their friends and siblings to value themselves as much as this group had taught them to do. Their discussion led to a team of eight girls deciding to explore opportunities to give back to others the care and confidence they had received from one another in the group.

As the group continued to shuffle possibilities, I thought of a teacher I'd met who had said she found girls this age ready and eager to serve. She said they experience a satisfaction and pride that helps them confront challenges they are facing. I suggested to the group that they look into opportunities to volunteer in some capacity that might help girls their age or younger.

The members loved the idea but soon discovered that it would be difficult to do it as a group, so they opted to individually choose one volunteer opportunity that would offer support and care to another girl or girls. Six of the group members committed to volunteer. Among the volunteer activities they individually chose were mentoring a third-grade girl in a reading program arranged by a school counselor and befriending a girl at school who was being bullied.

Sarah, one of the group members, decided to talk to her youth pastor about signing up for the youth mission project, Work Camp, which sends teams to repair low-income homes. Her parents and older brother had participated in Work Camp for several years, but Sarah had been too young and refused to "just tag along." Now, Sarah shared that the main reason she wanted to be a part of this project was to represent her dad, who had died a year before. She also hoped that her volatile relationship with her mother would heal as they worked together with the camp. She was now eager to "tag along."

Long after Work Camp was over and Sarah was in middle school, I received a letter from Sarah's mother. She was grateful that Sarah had become involved with a volunteer project. She wrote that the experience had healed a lot of hurt and anger they had experienced in their relationship and that, in some ways, it helped Sarah grieve her father's death. She went on to describe their experience:

"The team Sarah and I were assigned to work on was the home of twin six-year-old girls whose father had died the month before we arrived. The family now had a lot of debt and no financial stability. Their mother had cerebral palsy and was confined to a wheelchair, leaving the two girls on their own for care and entertainment."

She wrote that Sarah took responsibility for watching the twins as other members of the team worked on the home. "Sarah had been defiant, angry, and pulled-in since the death of her own father, but within a week, Sarah seemed transformed. I watched her come back to life as she connected with two little girls who had experienced the same loss as she had only a year ago. Since Work Camp, Sarah has continued to write letters and cards to the twins. She has even signed both of us up for the next Work Camp next summer. Whatever it was that turned her heart around, I want you to know it worked."

Sarah's experience reflects the profound transformation that can take place when girls connect to experiences that take them outside themselves and the circumstances of their lives. Choosing to volunteer gave Sarah not only the opportunity to turn her grief into an action that helped her heal but also a chance to give joy and hope to two young girls. In a way, Sarah became the wise elder in these girls' lives.

For the first time since her father's death, Sarah believed that her life mattered and that she could make a significant difference in her world. Her road map expanded to include a more confident and empathic self that previously had been out of reach.

Wise Connection Three: Nutrition

Talking to tweens about healthy choices can feel like walking a tightrope. You don't want to add to their already body image–preoccupied worries, yet at the same time, they need to understand that the choices they make every day have a profound effect on how they feel today and set the stage for a healthy future. Utilizing a wise mentor to guide your daughter's behaviors can help empower her to take control over her health.

Casey's Story: Healthy Choices

Steve and Sandra attended a parenting class I was facilitating. One evening after class, they approached me to talk about Casey, their youngest daughter. Sandra and Steve, who encourage their children (perhaps a little too much) to be physically healthy, had spent a lot of effort trying to convince Casey to be more conscious regarding the foods she ate. They were convinced she was turning into a couch potato and food junkie. Their efforts to get her to eat healthful foods and exercise bounced up against a budding adolescent who was not interested in her parents' advice. Needless to say, the more her parents wanted her to make healthy choices, the less Casey wanted it for herself. The push and pull left all parties frustrated and created the classic parent-adolescent power struggle.

It had become clear to them that their approach was not working and that perhaps an outsider like myself could speak with Casey and convince her that her parents were trying to help and she needed to listen. I explained that if I were Casey, having to see a therapist because she wasn't exercising or eating organic snacks might seem like a punishment.

I suggested that instead of trying to force her to eat healthy foods, this was the perfect time to help Casey discover more about nutrition and begin taking responsibility and ownership of her self-care. Steve and Sandra were interested and invested in supporting their daughter, especially at a time when Casey was concerned about entering a new middle school the following year. As we explored ways they could approach Casey, I suggested they consider planning a ritual at her next birthday that would focus on helping Casey take more responsibility of her nutrition and self-care. This would let her feel in control rather than controlled by her parents—a powerful lesson for all girls. I recommended they contact a nutritionist who had spoken to groups I had facilitated in the past. I explained that girls responded well to Donna and liked learning ways to stay fit while also staying healthy. Casey's parents were on board, relieved that they did not have to take on this responsibility alone.

A few months prior to her tenth birthday, the family began discussing ways to celebrate Casey's birthday. She would have her usual sleepover party with friends, but in addition to that party, Casey had agreed to see a nutritionist. After her first appointment with Donna, she was hooked and asked if she could join a teen health class her nutritionist facilitated. Her parents agreed, and Casey's group went on to meet once a month for a year.

Without any prodding, Casey began making a list of foods she wanted her parents to purchase at the store and often went with them to pick out the items she needed to prepare her school lunches. By working with an outside resource, Casey was able to take charge of obtaining new information and take ownership of her own health.

Having Casey's birthday on the heels of her budding interest in nutrition helped make Steve and Sandra's choice of the ritual to mark their daughter's birthday easy. They surprised Casey by taking her to a private cooking lesson, where they joined her in preparing a healthy, delicious meal. Afterward, Casey, her parents, and the chef sat and enjoyed a few hours of fun conversation, topped off with Casey's favorite dessert, prearranged by the chef herself.

Introducing an outside resource who could teach Casey about nutrition and self-care resulted in Steve, Sandra, and Casey getting what they wanted—a stronger connection—while at the same time helping to build Casey's sense of independence and accountability in keeping her body healthy.

Using a ritual to help your daughter connect to and interact with wise mentors at this age has the power to further solidify her foundation, thus shaping the roles she will try on outside of her family. With their dreams, self-care, and ambitions bolstered by strength, courage, and, most importantly, possibilities beyond what will be modeled by their peers and pop culture, these connections develop into a road map for your daughter when she faces complex situations.

Chapter 8

Ritual Four: Staying Connected

✸ Age Eleven ✸

Too often, the girls I work with think their parents do not "get them," much less make an effort to understand what they are going through. Recently, I led a session with a group of middle school girls in which we discussed how to communicate better with parents. Among their comments on the subject were the following:

> "I sometimes wonder if my mom is really listening to me when I talk to her. She is either texting, scrolling through her emails, talking on her phone, or checking Facebook. And they think *I* have a problem!"

"I always feel like no one in my house really cares what I have to say, so I figure, why bother?"

"I've learned that what I think or feel really doesn't matter. My parents always say that I'm just going through a stage and I'll get over it soon, or they laugh and tell me my hormones are starting to show. What am I supposed to do with that?"

When I share similar comments with parents, their response is typically, "Of course I care what my daughter feels and thinks! She should know that." Parents want to believe it's that simple, that their daughter knows without proof that they care about what she has to say, but it isn't that easy.

The Meaning of Staying Connected

Even though they may not show it, girls want to be validated by and connected to their parents, especially during these preadolescent years. When they transition into their tween years, they are more open to sharing thoughts and emotions than they will be as teenagers. They still want to talk about what is going on in their lives and to hear what their parents have to say. If they learn that they are free to share what is on their minds and that their parents care, they have little reason to hide their thoughts.

Around the age of eleven, when middle school typically starts, this openness gradually closes and daughters start sharing less with their parents and more with their peers. During this developmental transition, girls struggle to hold onto their voice, often afraid to disagree or stand up for themselves. They shift from wanting approval from parents to seeking validation from peers, which often leads to second-guessing their own opinions and surrendering to those of others to gain approval. To avoid rejection, girls begin to yield their values and minimize their needs.

I have found that at this stage, the ease of communication between daughters and parents greatly influences whether girls will choose to speak out, shut down, compromise their views, or submit to the pressures they will inevitably face. Active listening by parents—which requires intentionally carving out time to listen to their daughter's thoughts and emotions—helps girls to express and make sense of their confusion. By engaging in thoughtful conversations with your daughter, you demonstrate that you honor what matters to her, leading her to value her own wisdom and ultimately to have the courage to stand up to outside pressures. If her experience is that you minimize or object to her opinions, emotions, or exploration of thoughts, she will seek outside resources to fulfill this need, however ineffectively.

This is once again illustrated by *The Wonderful Wizard of Oz*. Dorothy's journey represents that of many girls who search for someone to listen to their needs and care about what matters to them. Feeling invisible and believing their needs or concerns are not important to their families, girls—like Dorothy—are likely to find other paths, following anyone who promises to listen and fulfill their dreams.

In the story, three keys to the journey—intelligence, heart, and courage—are symbolized by the Scarecrow, the Tin Man, and the Lion. They represent the internal strength needed to liberate the forces within Dorothy to stand up to bullies and outside pressures that steer girls away from home—their true selves—rather than closer to it.

It is up to you to help your daughter gain the strength that comes from feeling connected to home. When she talks about crushes on boys, friend-related fears, and other social pressures, be curious about what she is saying, even if it sounds irrational or unimportant to you. Respecting her concerns provides vital support to your daughter as she integrates her old life and behaviors with the unfamiliar territory she is entering. In this way, you offer her the reassurance and safety to explore her thoughts, to think things through, and to connect to what she truly believes in.

Making the shift to listening more and lecturing less builds a bridge that connects your two worlds rather than walls that separate them. Parents I work with want to do just that but struggle to know how. They often ask me, "How can we let our daughter know we care and are concerned about what goes on in her world without seeming to approve of it all?"

Mahatma Gandhi once advised, "Be the change you want to see in your world." If you want a strong bridge between you and your daughter, one that can endure tough conversations and conflict throughout her adolescent years, the time to start stabilizing your reactions is now. The ritual described in this chapter demonstrates how to accomplish that.

When your daughter is behaving irrationally, impulsively, or reactively, you won't be able to help if you behave in similar ways. Rather than becoming angry, fearful, or judgmental, you can instead learn to tolerate the tensions these conversations evoke through greater understanding and curiosity. That will bring resolution rather than a power struggle that can weaken your relationship.

In a world where many youths and parents spend more time watching screens and being plugged in than connecting with and understanding one another, listening has become endangered. Waiting for a teachable moment doesn't work at this juncture in your daughter's life—you must create them to ensure that they happen.

When your daughter does talk with you, stop what you are doing and listen. If you can't at that moment, explain why, then reassure her that you want to hear her thoughts. Arrange a time to talk and make sure you follow through within a day. When that time comes, return to what she wanted to discuss and focus on listening in order to *understand*, not to agree. Preteens are savvy, and if your daughter senses you aren't really interested in what she is saying now, she won't expect you to ever be interested. And before you insert your opinions, pause and take a breath; your thoughts matter, but not until later in the conversation. If your daughter trusts that you are *with* her and invested in her world, she is more likely to continue to open up to you.

The Staying Connected ritual helps you to be intentional about listening. It focuses on how you can help your daughter cultivate her communication with you and, later on, with others. You will learn to:

- Listen to your daughter's heart and help her value her own instincts.
- Respect and pay attention to her thoughts, even if they do not make sense to you. Try to understand them from an eleven-year-old girl's point of view.
- Listen to understand rather than to judge, avoiding "yes" or "no" responses.
- Ask questions to help her explore alternatives and consequences, developing her ability to make good decisions.
- Engage in dialogues that demonstrate your support and encouragement of her speaking up to you and to others.

Ritual Four: Staying Connected, Part One

Step One: Make Time

Find a time when you and your daughter can be alone and uninterrupted. In your own words, explain the following: You want to understand her experiences in her preteen and teenage years and to guide her through them in a helpful way. To do that, good communication between you two is essential. This is often difficult for you because until now, your role was to teach and make the decisions. But as she matures and grows more independent, you are learning that your role is to help her explore her opinions, guide her as she makes healthy choices, and be more curious about what she wants and ways she can take more responsibility. Let her know that you want to hear and understand her opinions, interests, and concerns. Tell her that you want her help as you practice doing this, then tell her that you have learned a way of communicating that can help you both as she becomes more independent.

Girls this age are very receptive to being told that their parents want to understand. Tweens and teens are biologically and neurologically wired to desire this response from their parents. Rebellion is not as extreme when this desire and need is met. In spite of whatever their first reaction is, deep inside, they will welcome your interest in their opinions and in helping them become more independent.

Step Two: Pick a Place

Ask your daughter to choose a comfortable, familiar place where the two (or three, if both parents are involved) of you can sit and talk. This should be a quiet spot away from family and activities where conversation can be confidential. Make a date and time to meet. Make sure the sitting area allows you to face one another.

Step Three: Start the Conversation

Explain to your daughter that the technique you are about to practice will help you, the parent, listen to and better understand her thoughts and opinions. Admit that you know this new way of communicating will be very different and maybe even uncomfortable for both of you at first. Reassure her that this discomfort wears off as the conversation broadens.

Step Four: Teach the Rules

Explain that in this conversation, each of you will listen not necessarily to agree but to understand what the other is saying. Each of you commits to not reacting, responding, or interrupting until the speaker has completely finished sharing what they have to say.

Go on to explain that the one speaking will say a few sentences and stop so the one listening can reflect back, in their own words, what the speaker said. The listener will not respond with opinions or judgments—no eye-rolling, huffing, or other passive ways to show disagreement with or rejection of the other's thoughts. Explain that this is the time for each of you, as listener, to really key into what the other is saying. Remember, if your daughter can trust you to listen to the stuff on the surface, she may trust you enough to talk about deeper things.

Answer any questions she has about the technique.

Step Five: Ask and Listen

Next, begin the conversation by asking your daughter, "What is it like having [me/us] as your [mom/dad/parents]?" Ask her to say only two or three sentences at a time so you can reflect them back accurately.

Be patient as she thinks about her answer. This may be the first time she's considered the question. When she speaks, just listen—*do not react*—and then repeat back to her what you *heard* her say, not what you *think* about it. This is not the time for you to respond. Being fully present to your daughter means practicing the discipline of listening solely to understand her. Listen through the ears of your eleven-year-old daughter, not your own.

Step Six: Validate

When your daughter is finished, ask, "Is there anything else?" If she says no, validate her thoughts. Acknowledge the truth in what she has said; however, validating and acknowledging do not mean that you agree. You simply make it clear that you have heard and understood how she feels, thinks, and experiences her life with you. When she describes your behaviors that you are aware of, take ownership of them. In doing so, you model courage, honesty, responsibility, and openness to change. This also teaches you more about your daughter, helping you to more effectively guide her and to improve your connection with her.

Step Seven: Make It Matter

When your daughter has finished answering your question, tell her, in your own words, the following: "I want to support and help you right where you are now and as you grow and develop into the smart, kind, and beautiful daughter that I know you are. But having listened to you and being more aware of how life is for you, I think there are some things you might need from me or perhaps want me to do differently. I'm not sure I can, but I would like to try. So can you tell me how I might respond to you differently or what I can do to help you get what you need?"

Allowing her to respectfully tell you her feelings and ideas and asking what she needs from you are powerful moments for you and your daughter. In this interaction, you model for her that it is safe to talk about things with you and that you are willing to put aside your agenda and reactions long enough to understand her inner life. If she learns this early on, then later, when adolescence complicates her life even more, it will be natural and safe for her to discuss her life with you.

This ritual begins to develop your daughter's self-exploration of skills and her connection to her inner world, perhaps without her being aware of it. She will discover what she feels, her reactions and impulses to these feelings and thoughts, and, most importantly, what she wants to do to create the outcomes she wants rather than those she fears. The ritual demonstrates to her that you, her parents, are willing to hear her out and help her make sense of it all. When you listen to understand, you model your value for and interest in your daughter's thoughts and feelings, thus teaching *her* to value and trust them. This exchange builds the courage she will need in the future to step out and do what she knows is best for her. With your daughter connected to her heart, believing that self-knowledge matters and having the courage to speak her thoughts, trusting that they will be validated by her parents, your daughter is more likely to expect this from future relationships.

Rebecca's Story: Opening the Conversation

Ed, a single dad, was concerned about his daughter Rebecca's entry into middle school. He had heard horror stories about how bullied, manipulated, eager to please, and rebellious kids become when they enter sixth grade. He said that after his wife's death when his daughter was nine years old, Rebecca became reserved and seemed to lose her confidence and outspoken spirit. He had become overprotective and controlling and was now concerned that Rebecca would not be able to stand up to the pressures of middle school. He wanted to help her spread her wings but was horrified by what that might look like. His fear of losing her blocked his ability to relax his grip on her life.

Ed realized that the best way to begin was to open communication between him and Rebecca. This would demand self-reflection and risk on his part, but without it, his fears would sabotage

Rebecca's independence and self-confidence and the strong relationship between them. With my guidance, Ed decided to try the Staying Connected ritual, following the steps as outlined. Later, he described how it went.

Ed: Rebecca, what is it like having me as your dad these days?

Rebecca: It's great, Dad.

Ed: Great? How is it great?

Rebecca: We do a lot of stuff together. You always take me to California Pizza on Thursdays after gymnastics, and you make awesome waffles on Sunday. Just like Mom made.

Ed [reflecting what Rebecca had said]: So, you like us going for pizza after your gymnastic practices, and you think it's pretty cool that I can make waffles like Mom did. I'm glad you enjoy those times we share. Are there other things about having me as a dad that you like or wish were different?

Rebecca: Well, since you are asking—and you said you wanted me to be honest—I will tell you something I wish you would do differently. When you do this, it makes me really mad, and then I really wish Mom were here.

Ed: Go ahead; I'm listening.

Rebecca [hesitantly]: When you keep reminding me that I need to do my homework and checking to see if I did it, that really gets on my nerves. It's like you don't trust me.

Ed: So you don't like it when I check up on you.

Rebecca: Yeah, Dad, and it doesn't stop there. When I'm in my room on the phone or computer or hanging out with my friends, you keep coming into my room. You're always asking me if I'm OK or asking if I need something, when I just wish you would go away.

Ed [working to avoid reacting]: It sounds like you're mad.

Rebecca: I am! And remember, you asked for this.

Ed: I did, so go on.

Rebecca: Dad, you act as if you don't trust me. I like hanging out in my room, talking with my friends. I don't want to hang out with you all the time. I love you and I like it when we do things, but there's stuff I want to do without you.

Ed: It seems as if you want to have more time by yourself and with your friends without me popping in. When I do that, it really bugs you.

Rebecca: Yes! And just the other day, when I asked you if I could go over to my new friend's house, you asked a thousand questions. What's up with that? Sometimes it's easier to just stay here and not make new friends.

Ed: So, sometimes you feel as if I don't trust you because I'm always checking on things and asking questions. It sounds like you feel you can't have any privacy or alone time without me barging in.

Rebecca [in a softer tone]: Yeah, Dad, that's it. It's not that I don't want to hang out with you, but I just need time with my friends without you wanting to know all about it.

Ed: Rebecca, I think I understand. So, can you help me remember this when you feel like I'm intruding or hovering too much? I guess I need my daughter to help me out with this.

Rebecca: OK. So after I finish my homework, what about you just letting me have an hour in my room without checking on me?

Ed: That sounds fair. Let's try it for a month and see how it goes. And when I forget, just remind me. It's a habit and it might take time for me to remember, but your job is to remind me.

Next, using that same process of listening to understand, the ritual continues, this time giving your daughter the opportunity to develop listening skills to understand you, the parent. It also gives you the opportunity to remember and describe what life was like for you when you were your daughter's age. This exercise helps you connect more deeply to what your daughter is feeling.

Ritual Four: Staying Connected, Part Two

Step One: Reverse Roles

Now that your daughter has answered your question, it's her turn to question you. Ask her to ask the question, "What was it like for you when you were my age?"

Think back to when you were eleven years old, and remember what you looked like, things you enjoyed, your social environment, what you disliked, and your interactions with your parents, peers, and teachers. Share these with your daughter, telling her what they were like for you, how you felt about yourself and your parents, what you wanted life to be more like, and what you liked about your life. Say only two or three sentences at a time. If this conversation triggers painful memories for you, pause and take a few deep breaths before going forward. (If you have memories that are not appropriate for your daughter to hear at her age, then it is best to generalize your childhood experience rather than offer descriptive details.)

Step Two: Reflecting Back and Validating

Ask your daughter to reflect back to you what she heard you say, without judgment or commentary. Then she can ask if there is more you can tell her. Continue this dialogue until you both feel that you have completed your talk. When you are finished, your daughter will close the dialogue by validating what she heard you say.

Ed's Story: A New Kind of Conversation

A few weeks later, Ed and his daughter reversed roles, with Rebecca being the listener and Ed being the speaker.

Rebecca: So, Dad, what was it like for you when you were my age?

Ed: Well, my dad died when I was five, and my mother remarried someone I never felt connected to or liked very much. When I was your age, eleven, my stepfather died and my mother was left to manage our lives alone. It was just her and me.

Rebecca: Wow, Dad, I knew about your dad dying, but I had forgotten about your second dad dying, too. And that you and your mom were left alone.

Ed: Yeah. And my grandfather, the only male in my life who ever made me feel loved, was sick, so my mother had to travel to take care of him. She was always afraid something would happen to me when she was away, so she insisted that I go directly to a neighbor's house every day when I got off the bus. Miss Molly was a kind but very strict elderly lady. Old Miss Molly.

Rebecca: That must have been a drag, having to go home and stay with some old lady who probably wouldn't let you do anything.

Ed: Yep, nothing but homework. Even when I didn't have homework, she would make things up for me to study or read out of the newspaper. I hated it.

Rebecca: So you couldn't do anything but homework, and she even made you read stupid stuff out of the newspaper when you didn't have other work. Boy, your life was worse than mine. At least I get to come home to my house and hang with my things.

Ed: No kidding. My mother was very overprotective and made me feel like a dog on a chain. It wasn't just at this age—even when I got older, she held me back out of fear that I would get hurt. She always said it was for my own good, but she had such a tight grip on my life that I didn't have my own life. I still get angry thinking about that.

Rebecca: So, Dad, you got angry, too, about the stupid things your parents did—well, your mom. Maybe you felt kind of like I do, but you had it way worse.

(Ed was becoming aware of anger he had not thought of for years. He told himself he couldn't lose it in front of Rebecca. After he took a breath or two, the conversation continued.)

Rebecca: What was that like for you, Dad?

Ed: I felt alone a lot, Rebecca, and trapped. I wasn't allowed to have any adventures, play sports, or hang out with any of my friends. I loved playing football and, believe it or not, I was pretty good at it.

Rebecca [smiling]: Dad, I'm really sorry you couldn't do that. That just was not fair!

Ed: I know, sweetie. I couldn't wait until I could go to middle school and play on a school team. And I did make the team, but halfway through the season, my mother made me quit because she was afraid I would get hurt riding the athletic bus home. After that, I withdrew from my friends and kind of watched my life go by. I felt pretty helpless to do anything about it. From that time throughout my middle school years, it was Miss Molly and me.

Rebecca: Gosh, Dad, that's awful. It wasn't fair.

Ed: Nope, Rebecca, it wasn't. Just like it isn't fair that I'm always checking on you and get upset when you spend too much time in your room or with your friends on the computer and phone.

Rebecca: Yeah, you're right. But you aren't that hard, and I don't feel trapped like you did. I just get angry sometimes when you stay on my back too much. I need space that's mine without you always wanting to know about it or be there.

Ed: I know. I get it now. That's what I wanted from my mother. Luckily, when I entered high school, she let go a little. I started playing football, and she even didn't freak out the time I was carried off the field on a stretcher.

Rebecca: What happened to change your mom's mind?

Ed: I'm not really sure. As you would say, she might have taken a chill pill. But who knows? What mattered was that she did somehow, and I got to play ball.

Rebecca: I'm glad you finally got your adventure, too . . . maybe like you're going to try to let me have mine?

Ed: For sure, kid; for sure.

This ritual builds a solid foundation from which girls can speak their truth without the fear of being criticized, rejected, shamed, or minimized. Parents learn how to keep the dialogue open and to listen with understanding rather than with agreement or judgment. When you demonstrate that you understand and care about your daughter's opinions by giving her opportunities to explain them respectfully, she learns to expect that from her outside world. Having the right to an opinion and valuing one's feelings and needs will build a significant framework of self-confidence and worth. When your daughter asks with interest about your experience of life at her age, you and she discover that the divide between the two generations isn't as great as you had imagined.

Learning to parent from the banks of the river rather than by jumping into your daughter's boat and taking over the navigation is challenging for both you and your daughter. It is at this stage in the rituals, in the midst of holding on while gently letting go, that you can create safe and supportive boundaries that allow your daughter to meander, struggle, and strengthen her sense of self on her own—though you'll never be too far behind if she needs help.

Chapter 9

Ritual Five: Dropping Inside

❀ Age Twelve ❀

At the age of twelve, your daughter officially enters her adolescent years, emotionally and physically opening the door to the most dynamic years of her life. Her body and mind demand change and independence. According to Daniel Siegel, hormones are not the only cause of these changes. He writes, "One of the most powerful myths surrounding adolescence is that raging hormones cause teenagers to 'go mad' or 'lose their minds.' That's simply false. Hormones do increase during this period, but it is not the hormones that determine what goes on in adolescence. We now know that what adolescents experience is primarily the result of changes in the development of the brain."[1]

It is normal and necessary for girls to try on many different roles during their preteen and teenage years. As they chisel through these experiences, they excavate undeveloped parts of themselves and strengthen the qualities they already have. In the best circumstances, this provides a solid foundation to support and stabilize their personal evolution and growth. Rituals One through Four help families support this foundation, preparing the girls for this new stage—a stage when parents and daughters must embrace change, not fight it.

As girls experiment with a variety of identities to discover who they are outside of their families, they will be influenced by pressures that encourage them to either believe in themselves or surrender who they are. Media and pop culture lure them in many directions other than toward their authentic, independent selves, often conveying the message that girls have to abandon innocence in order to be socially savvy and sophisticated. Social media and cyber relationships provide an artificial sense of power that ultimately leaves girls feeling alone. Girls I work with report feeling overwhelmed by pressures to perform academically, socially, and sexually. Many turn to soft drugs, drinking, or cutting as a relief for their internalized stress.

The fact is, every adolescent girl will encounter and be influenced by role models and peer pressure. Instead of trying to avoid that reality, parents can recognize that this is normal and choose to focus on providing their daughter with the tools to support her inner self when overwhelmed by pressures and stressors that outside influences bring into her life.

The Meaning of Dropping Inside

Teaching Mindfulness

In spite of many myths and ongoing jokes that blame raging hormones for the radical behavior changes and mood swings in teenagers, new research helps us understand that it is not hormones alone that dictate these years—your daughter's developing, active brain is in charge. Siegel writes:

> From around the age of twelve to age twenty-four, there is a burst of growth and maturation taking place as never before in our lives. Understanding the nature of these changes can help us create a more positive and productive life journey. This period in the adolescent's life is one with the most power for courage and creativity. Life is on fire when we hit our teens. And these changes are not something to avoid, but to encourage. While the adolescent years may be challenging, the changes in the brain that help support the unique emergence of the adolescent mind can create qualities in us that help us not only during our adolescent years, if used wisely, but also as we enter adulthood and live fully as an adult. How we navigate the waters of adolescence—as young individuals on the journey or adults walking with them—can help guide the ship that is our life into treacherous places or into exciting adventures. The decision is ours. That decision has a direct impact on how we'll live the rest of our lives.[2]

I often remind parents and girls I work with that choices they make will either take them one step closer to what they truly want or one step away from it. The power of change, as Mahatma Gandhi reminds us, lies within the decisions we make from one moment to the next. During these radical, changing years of transition from tween and teen, parents can choose to pause, think through the outcome they most desire, and then build connections and responses that lead them in that direction.

Teen girls will often feel irritable, angry, and self-conscious when physical, emotional, and academic pressures are placed on them before they are physiologically or psychologically ready. Educators and parents see this played out in more aggressive risk-taking, impulsive behaviors, and reduced ability to focus in the classroom and at home. Symptoms of anxiety and stress among girls I work with have sharply increased over the past thirty years. Being ready to respond in ways that help your daughter work through these changes rather than irrationally react to them is a choice that has the power to change the path you and your daughter will travel throughout adolescence and the outcome each of you will experience.

With forty percent of teens today reporting that they feel stressed out and anxious almost every day, introducing girls to the practice of mindfulness is a crucial tool. Mindfulness is a practice that helps girls pause to drop inside of themselves long enough to focus attention on what is going on in the moment. By learning not to judge each moment or make up stories about it, girls begin to shift out of the negative thinking that can sabotage their best intentions. In fact, mindfulness teaches girls to replace judgment with acceptance and kindness. The practice of mindfulness develops qualities that regulate girls' inner worlds, which are often filled with stress, worries, and fears of rejection. Rather than getting caught up in fears or negative chatter, girls who practice mindfulness can think more clearly before responding to daily events. This gives them more control over external pressures rather than being controlled by them.

In an excerpt from *Building Emotional Intelligence: Techniques to Cultivate Inner Strength in Children*, Linda Lantieri found the following:

Many of us who have been teaching these skills [meaning mindfulness practices] to children have been heartened by some of the changes we've noticed. For example, Kimberly Schonert-Reichl, from the University of Columbia in Canada, observed that children who were taught a mindfulness technique similar to the one in this book were "less aggressive; less oppositional toward teachers; more attentive in class; and reported more positive emotions including more optimism." Susan Smalley, director of the Mindfulness Awareness Research Center at UCLA, also found positive results from teaching these techniques to teenagers with attention deficit hyperactivity disorder (ADHD). She found that learning mindfulness techniques reduced their anxiety and increased their ability to focus. . . . When mindfulness is learned young, these practices decrease stress, attention deficit issues, depression, anxiety, and hostility in children, while also benefiting their health, well-being, social relationships, and academic performance.[3]

Research has long established the effectiveness and success of Mindfulness-Based Stress Reduction (MBSR), developed by Jon Kabat-Zinn, in hospitals, schools, and social and mental health facilities. Having studied MBSR, I regularly use it in my work with girls. I have found it to be one of the most successful ways of helping girls cope with anxiety, stress, impulse control, and irrational reactions triggered by fear and pressure to perform. I teach girls to use these simple practices while at their desks, at parties, in hallways and bathrooms, and in their beds at night when they can't get to sleep. Some have taught the practices to close friends. Parents have been relieved to see that their daughters can depend on these nonintrusive and nonaddictive practices rather than on unhealthy coping strategies and behaviors.

The girls who learn mindfulness report greater ability to manage anxiety related to taking tests, dating, and relationships. Before learning mindfulness, they were debilitated by stress and out-of-control negative thinking. After, they felt greater calmness and reduced emotional reactivity.

In this chapter, I outline four mindfulness practices that have had positive results in my own practice and that of many other experts in the field. Experiencing all four is optimal for broadening your daughter's awareness of ways to manage stress, anxiety, and pressures. At a minimum, I recommend that you try to incorporate two of the four practices of mindfulness into your daughter's life at this age. These practices can be turned into rituals for your daughter's twelfth year, as detailed later in this chapter.

Mindfulness Practice One: Breathing

In this practice, the breath is the object of the girl's concentration. Focusing on the breath anchors her mind and helps to stabilize anxious thoughts that take her attention away from the present moment and rational thinking. Bringing full attention to the breath relaxes her body and mind, allowing them to work together.

Elizabeth's Story: Gaining Control

Elizabeth performed well in school and kept a 4.3 weighted GPA throughout high school, but she came to me to discuss her anxiety about taking the SATs. She had frozen each time she took them and couldn't complete the test. After four tries, she was desperate. I suggested we explore working with mindful breathing techniques to help her relax and ease her fears of failure rather than letting them shut her down.

I explained and taught her the practice of Mindfulness-Based Stress Reduction. After four sessions, Elizabeth went into her fifth try at taking the exam and nailed it! She reported that every time she felt her body getting anxious or she became aware that she wanted to run outside, she picked up her pencil, pretending to read the exam, and practiced the techniques of mindful breathing. An example of the breathing technique Elizabeth used was the following:

> Slowly breathing, Elizabeth focused her attention on the breath moving up through her body on inhalation and slowly releasing the breath through exhalation. She imagined her breath as soft wave moving up onto the shore when she inhaled then moving back out to the ocean when she exhaled. Each time the wave came in up through her body, she accepted that she was anxious about passing the test. On the exhalation, Elizabeth told herself, "But if I look at just the facts, I know I'm smart enough to pass. So I'll just let my fears wash back into the ocean with my breath." Watching the breath move out of her body on her exhalation, Elizabeth felt her body relax and was able to let fears go.

Focusing on her breath rather than her fear enabled Elizabeth to move forward with the questions, completing the exam. It wasn't that the panic had disappeared but that Elizabeth finally had the tools to not let the panic take control.

Betsy's Story: Dealing with Bullies

A twelve-year-old client named Betsy told me that she had been skipping a class she dreaded. Throughout the semester, several students in the class had bullied her to the extent that she was fearful of speaking when called on, even if she knew the answer. Her anxiety grew until she felt panic when she walked to the class. Thinking it was her only way out, Betsy began to cut class and forge notes from her parents explaining her absences. I was asked to facilitate an intervention.

Betsy and I began working to build a repertoire of breathing exercises she could use when she started to feel panic about entering the class. With the bullies reprimanded and Betsy's ability to calm the panic when triggered, she was able to think and respond more rationally. Going to class took on a new association, and Betsy maintained a B average and successfully checked the class off her list.

Mindfulness Practice Two: Body Scan — Staying Awake to Your Body

The Body Scan is a mindfulness practice that trains the mind to be aware of and sensitive to what's going on in the body. It leads to compassion for and acceptance of one's body.

Preadolescent and teenage girls struggle with a negative body image and spend an exorbitant amount of time trying to look "perfect," yet they also spend hours in front of mirrors engaging in negative talk. The Body Scan helps girls to appreciate and accept their bodies. Mindfully connecting to their bodies, girls are encouraged to accept their imperfections.

Taking this time to settle into their bodies and calm their minds gives girls a way to decompress and disconnect from the pressures that weigh on them. Today, many girls seldom drop into REM sleep because their bodies are on alert for the next text on their cell phones. Girls I work with report that when they start their sleep with a Body Scan, their racing mind relaxes and their body's need for sound sleep takes over.

Paying attention as the mind scans and connects to the body helps girls develop a keen awareness of what their bodies are feeling and needing. At the same time, the breathing techniques help calm their bodies. This is a powerful way to help your daughter work with her body rather than be angry with it. In addition, for girls who struggle going to sleep due to anxiety, the body scan is a very effective practice just before bedtime.

The Body Scan is not practiced specifically to help your daughter relax or fall asleep; it is designed to help her stay "awake" to her body. Developing awareness of what is going on in her body helps her develop an appreciation for and attentiveness to the care of her body. The secondary benefit of relaxation comes from the steady focus of the mind on the body. You can introduce this practice so your daughter can do it right in her home. It might even be fun and helpful for you to practice this along with your daughter.

Before starting, you need to download or purchase recorded guided meditations that include the Body Scan or follow the instructions in the Appendix of this book. I recommend researching and choosing Body Scan recordings by experienced professionals in the field of mindfulness. I highly recommend listening to recordings by Jon Kabat-Zinn. Gina Biegel is an additional resource; she adapted MBSR for teens and has developed the Stress Reduction Workbook for Teens *and the audio CD and MP3 recording* Meditation Practices to Reduce Stress and Promote Well-Being. *Another option is to find good mindfulness apps available on iTunes, YouTube, and Headspace that are easy for preteens and teens to have at their fingertips. There are many other options, like DVDs and MP3 downloads.*

It is important that you first practice the Body Scan before introducing it to your daughter. After guiding her in the Scan, encourage her to practice it several times a month. When practiced often, it becomes an easy and convenient tool for when your daughter needs to relax.

Group Story: The Need for Sleep

Several years ago, I facilitated a clinical group of middle school girls once a week after school. One afternoon, when they had been doing mindfulness practices for a few months, they complained about being tired and stressed from taking exams all week. We decided it was the perfect time to practice the Body Scan.

They tossed their mats on the floor, giving each other plenty of space to relax. I dimmed the light to make it easier for them to shift into a quiet space. They closed their eyes and took a few minutes to shift their focus and attention from school to their bodies. After a couple of deep breaths, I asked them to begin focusing their attention on their toes and their breath moving around their toes, relaxing every small bone and tiny muscle.

Before I could get them to imagine their breath moving into other parts of their bodies, four of the six girls were asleep. When I had finished the Body Scan, the fifth girl was asleep. One girl remained awake, and she and I had an interesting conversation about her upcoming classes while the others slept even after the Body Scan was over. They learned how to relax when their bodies were desperate for rest. The Body Scan helped these girls become more aware of what their bodies needed—in this case, sleep.

Mindfulness Practice Three: Yoga

Yoga has been increasing in popularity in recent years, so many people have at least a basic understanding of what it entails. At its core, yoga facilitates a connection between mind and body through breathing practices, body positions, and meditation.

Many girls who have grown up with at least a rudimentary understanding of yoga find it a comfortable first step on the journey to mindfulness. Through the practice of yoga, girls learn the importance of taking time to unwind, relax, and release stress. They also become more in tune with their bodies. Increasingly, yoga studios, fitness centers, and recreation departments are offering classes specifically designed for tweens and teens.

By incorporating yoga into Hannah's twelfth birthday ritual, her family introduced mindfulness to her daughter and her friends. Her story is told later in this chapter.

Mindfulness Practice Four: Connections to the Natural World

When youths become more connected to, appreciative of, and educated about their environment, they develop a greater consciousness of and respect for keeping their environment healthy and creating the conditions necessary for the well-being of their physical and psychological health.

Electronic screens and devices are in danger of desensitizing us to a connection with nature. Time in nature is an easy and inexpensive way to help your daughter cultivate an awareness of the natural life around her. Listening to birds, experiencing the crunch of crisp, dry leaves under her feet, or pausing long enough to feel the warmth of the sun on her face helps her engage and connect to the natural world around her. A silent walk in nature allows mind and body to be in the moment—hopefully without Instagraming along the way! This practice strengthens her ability to be present and attuned to her surroundings—whether nature or social groups—and to develop a deeper connection to the effect they have on her.

Is there a family member, grandparent, uncle, aunt, or friend who enjoys hiking, bird-watching, or walking in nature? These are resources you can utilize to help you practice this exercise in the mindfulness ritual. Other outings might include a camping trip, a visit to a zoo or aquarium, canoeing, kayaking, or a walk on the beach. Consider the opportunities available to you that fit your daughter's interests and plan something that she'll find enjoyable and meaningful, as in Emma's story later in this chapter.

Breathing, meditation, and mindfulness practices help your daughter build her foundation as she works to become more connected to her inner self and her new landscape. The mindfulness principles also present a wonderful opportunity for parents, who can incorporate mindfulness as a ritual for their daughter's twelfth year. It can offer her effective ways to manage her anxiety, fears, and stress and be a starting point for including mindfulness in her life moving forward.

Ritual Five: Dropping Inside

While I encourage parents to introduce mindfulness practices in their daughter's life independent of any occasion, I have also seen families use mindfulness as part of developing powerful rituals for their daughters.

Hannah's Story: A Yoga Ritual

Hannah turned twelve years old and wanted to celebrate her birthday with friends. Her mother, who had marked her daughter's last three birthdays with rituals, wanted to continue the tradition and called me to ask for suggestions. Hannah and her mother agreed to a yoga-themed sleepover party. Guests and parents were informed that a basic yoga class would be part of the birthday party. Hannah's mother approached her own yoga instructor and explained that she wanted to hire her for an hour and a half to introduce a group of twelve-year-old females to the practice of yoga. Together, they formed a simple class that was age-appropriate for the beginners. The girls were advised to wear relaxed, simple clothing.

During the class, the yoga instructor taught the girls easy, practical stretches to relieve stress at school, at home, or right before going to bed. They practiced stretching exercises lying on the floor, sitting in chairs, and leaning against a wall. She reminded them that they needed nothing but their power of concentration. She also encouraged the girls to memorize a prayer, poem, scripture, or meaningful quote that would act as a mantra to soothe their anxiety when they became overstressed.

Before leaving, the instructor invited the girls to ask questions, share ideas, and talk about issues that were causing them stress. During their discussion, the teacher explained that stress is a physical symptom that signals them to wake up, take notice, and get serious about what is going on inside themselves. The girls learned that stress isn't their enemy but a friendly whisper reminding them to pay attention to the message their bodies are trying to communicate. She discussed the importance of unplugging from all electronic devices an hour before going to sleep and going to bed without their cell phones nearby. Technology, she explained, interferes with deep sleep, when the body and mind heals, rebuilds tissue and muscles, and strengthens the immune system.

The group yoga class was a huge success. Not only did the girls have fun and share a meaningful experience, but Hannah found the class so enjoyable she continues to take a yoga class at the YMCA.

Emma's Story: A Natural Connection

Emma's grandfather had been an avid bird-watcher for more than twenty years. He enjoyed packing up his truck and finding special spots in nature where he could go and watch birds. Emma had always admired him and felt they had a lot in common. He was introverted, enjoyed being outside, and was a little shy. Her parents suggested that he take Emma out bird-watching for her twelfth birthday and introduce her to his love for birds. He welcomed the invitation.

To mark the outing, Emma's grandfather presented her with a guidebook of local birds and her own pair of binoculars. After the outing, Emma shared that she became aware of how much patience she had to have to be still and focus on the birds. By doing so, Emma was exercising her mind to become more aware of the present moment and less caught up in her daily stresses—a skill she could use in her everyday life.

The practice of mindfulness is a cost-effective way to offer your daughter powerful tools that teach her an awareness of what is happening in her life, both internally and externally, and the ability to relax under stress. This awareness and skill help her to stay connected with her peers without compromising the connection she has with herself. These mindfulness practices teach your daughter to keep her heart and mind linked, guiding her in the direction of loving herself and cultivating self-acceptance—a gift that no glitter or glamour can replace.

Chapter 10

Ritual Six: The Return

❁ Age Thirteen ❁

Reviving the sacred tradition of rituals in the years leading up to your daughter's thirteenth birthday celebration makes a significant contribution in preparing her for this developmental transition. The six rituals work together to help her develop a clear sense of her secure, separate identity within and outside her family.

The sixth ritual strengthens your understanding of your daughter's inner world, instills curiosity in her exploration of the landscape beyond what she has known, and empowers her to draw on the teachings and connections that have been woven into her journey over the past several years. This final ritual integrates her heart, wisdom, and courage, each a vital part of her identity, to help her navigate her passage into her teen years.

The Meaning of the Return

Your daughter takes a leap of faith when she walks off the secure grounds of childhood and into her teen years. You also take a leap of faith as you expand boundaries and extend freedoms that are often scarier for you than for your daughter. Having faced fears and come together to strengthen your daughter's growth toward independence deepens her connection to family, especially you. You are setting the understanding that there is a home for her with a solid foundation. Through this strong connection, you ensure that your daughter knows without question that she can always return.

Today, tweens and teens are not emotionally, mentally, or physically ready to be completely separated from their families or communities to test their survival skills. However, as girls transition into their teen years, they can and will set goals that stretch them, meet pressures that force them to face fears, and make hard choices that call on self-knowledge and courage. Throughout your daughter's adolescence, she will come up against situations and people that make her uncomfortable. These may urge her to engage in activities her wisdom deems unsafe, which will create tension with her desire to be accepted. These are tough moments, when fears arise along with her willingness to risk and take chances.

In his work with rites of passage, James Hollis refers to the final two stages as the Ordeal and the Return. (In my work with girls, I combine each of these in the sixth ritual I refer to as the Return.) Hollis explains the Ordeal to be an extension of separation from the comforts and securities of home. This experience challenges the individual to face fears and obstacles that offer the opportunity to tap into the "strength within to meet the task without."[1]

In the Return, after experiencing the five rituals that mark a tween's rite of passage I have outlined in this book, your daughter reenters her community or family with a deeper sense of self-knowledge. Because of her current age, she remains dependent, but does so with a new awareness of and belief in her ability to risk standing before her fears and evaluating how she wants to work with them. At this stage in her journey, your daughter has taken a step away from full dependency and started to trust her wisdom and ability to survive challenges, thus consolidating her growth toward becoming independent.

It is crucial that your daughter has experiences that prepare her to know herself, make rational choices, and discern whether her fears are valid. These lessons help her cultivate the skill of listening to her inner voice and body to know the difference between "No, this isn't safe for me" and "I'm afraid I can't do this, but I still want to give it a try."

The rituals that culminate in the Return do this for your daughter. As she travels through them, guided by her parents and other important figures in her life, she develops the tools to listen to herself with wisdom and purpose.

In his book *Identity: Youth and Crisis*, developmental psychologist Erik H. Erikson discussed a concept central to understanding the essential and powerful journey this chapter speaks to. In trying to understand growth, Erikson worked with the epigenetic principle to focus on one's development within their social context. Believing that a child's biological development was influenced by environmental and cultural factors, Erikson presented stages of psychological development that were necessary to provoke growth and awareness, each forming one's distinct personality. Erikson believed that "the success or failure of each stage is in part determined by the success, or lack of success, in all previous stages."[2]

All of the rituals you created leading up to this thirteenth year have helped shape the young woman before you. She is not the same girl you remember from her first ritual at age eight. At the same time, she's probably not as different from that girl as she'd like to believe. The completion of this ritual closes a circle for her, one that began with important people from her life all around her. That's why returning to that foundation—her family—is so critical in planning this ritual.

Ritual Six: The Return

The Return is the final stage in your daughter's passage into her teen years. As she navigates the ritual, she encounters the Gathering, the Challenge, and the Blessing. The definition of each is explained in the following sections and illustrated with a story of how families planned and conducted the ritual.

Part One: The Gathering

Part one of this ritual acts as a reminder to your daughter that her family remains her support system, her cheering squad, and a safe landing place she can come back to for guidance and comfort. Returning to the circle—where her family waits to celebrate her achievements and growth and to reaffirm their commitment to guide, nurture, and support her—solidifies her security as she moves into adolescence.

In this ritual, your daughter shares with those closest to her how these rituals have shaped her life and what it has meant to her to become more aware of her family's support. She also listens as these special people share their observations of her growth.

After telling stories, catching up, and securing connections, the family (referred to as "the participants" in this ritual) prepares to leave for the next part, the Challenge.

Mary's Story: An Experience Revisited

Mary and her parents (whom you met in Chapter 5) returned to the cabin they had rented five years earlier when they marked the first ritual of Mary's tween years. Her parents had stayed in contact with everyone who had participated and now invited them back to the cabin to celebrate Mary's thirteenth birthday. Everyone except Mary's former babysitter was able to come for the day. The group planned to spend the night there and head out early the next morning for a surprise that would mark part two of Mary's final ritual: whitewater kayaking, guided by a professional instructor. Mary had wanted to try whitewater kayaking but had been fearful of trying it on her own.

Mary's parents had circled beach chairs around a campfire and set out the makings for s'mores. Mary's father spoke first, reflecting on the first time they had sat in this same circle, when Mary turned eight. Others joined in, sharing their memories of that experience. The stories shifted into their observations of how they now engage with and experience Mary. It was an exchange of affirmations and hilarious stories. At one point, Mary shared the difficulty she'd had during her middle school years and her relief that they would soon be over.

After the stories and laughter settled into quiet conversation and making s'mores, Mary's mother brought out a large bag and unfolded the Quilt of Courage Mary had started when she was eight. Everyone admired the quilt as Mary named each square, who had given it to her, and its significance. The time around the circle came to an end. Everyone settled in for the night and prepared to rise early and face the challenge of whitewater kayaking on the James River.

Part Two: The Challenge

Part two of this ritual invites your daughter to step out of her comfort zone and challenge herself to face difficult tasks, emotions, and experiences that give her opportunities to discover new responses and solutions. In doing so, she can experience the joy and pride of an accomplished goal that she wasn't sure she could manage or that felt beyond her reach.

It is important to consider your daughter's unique interests and physical, emotional, and mental capabilities when planning the Challenge. Ideally, the Challenge will be a stretch for her but ultimately one in which she will experience success. If she doesn't succeed in a traditional way, it is important that you, her parents, help her recognize the strength and courage she showed in making herself vulnerable to a new experience.

In planning the Challenge, it is important that the tasks associated with it fit within a family's specific financial parameters. Fortunately, there are various forms a Challenge can take. I've seen families create wonderful experiences for the Challenge, including hiking a difficult trail, having an authentic camping experience that emphasizes survival skills like gathering firewood and cooking outside, or even canoeing or kayaking.

The story below involves a group of girls but can just as easily be done with just your daughter.

Group Story: Outside Their Comfort Zone

Several years ago, I facilitated a yearlong group for eighth-grade girls with the aim of preparing them for high school and the issues they would face during that time. Their parents participated in three of the meetings. By the end of the year, all the girls had arrived at their thirteenth year and were proud they were no longer, as they said, "children."

For our final meeting, I suggested that we plan a day at Challenge and Discovery, an experiential learning and team-building organization located away from our usual meeting place. I explained that the experience would allow them to practice what they had worked on throughout the year, including facing fears, supporting one another, communicating, setting goals, setting boundaries, and owning their limitations. After discussing the details, the girls decided to do it. I suggested we invite their parents to go along. At first, they voiced an overwhelming "No," but later acquiesced, understanding that part of their growth had involved allowing their parents to help them work through issues rather than leaving them out.

Several weeks prior to the group's challenge, I asked the parents and girls to each write down one goal and one fear they had related to the girls entering their teen years. Challenge and Discovery worked with me in setting up a team-building challenge that related to the theme of setting goals.

Early on a rainy Saturday morning, the girls, their parents, and I left the safe and familiar group environment and traveled to Challenge and Discovery's Adventure Learning Center. When we arrived, our guide—a male instructor—greeted us with enthusiasm. We did warm-up games that gave everyone an opportunity to connect with the instructor and helped the parents to connect with their daughters in this new setting. After the warm-up, we were led to a large wooded area nearby. There, the group began a variety of low-to-the-ground problem-solving challenges, gradually working up to a high-challenge course that pushed several parents and daughters beyond their comfort zones.

Throughout these exercises, the group experienced heightened awareness and cooperation. The ever-increasing challenges required the group to work as a team. With each new challenge, the girls' mental, emotional, and physical resources were stretched. When parents struggled with challenges, the girls reached out and helped them. At other times, parents offered a hand to the daughters. The exchange of support felt easy and natural as the day progressed.

With the success of meeting each challenge, the girls discovered a deeper sense of confidence that lessened their fears. They also discovered that their parents at times needed help and support when the girls did not. Cheering parents on or lending a hand to one of their group members was a powerful experience.

The final challenge was called the "Leap of Faith," designed to give everyone the opportunity to face a fear and make a decision to let go of the fear's control in their lives. The guide explained that climbing up and jumping off a fifty-foot pole symbolized their transcendence of fear and their trust in themselves to be able to leap into the unfamiliar—their teen years. The measurement of success would be marked by their attempts to face their fear, name it, and own it, but not necessarily to climb the pole and jump off.

The instructor put a harness on each person and attached two safety ropes to the climber's harness. The group was divided into two teams. The climber's team held one of the safety ropes; the instructor held the second. The team's job was to release or tighten the rope as the climber directed. If the participant felt she was beginning to fall, she would yell to tighten the rope. If she needed more rope to climb higher, she would call for her team to loosen the rope. Team cohesiveness was essential, and the girl climbing had to decide if she would trust the team and, most importantly, herself. Once the climber reached the top of the pole, she had to stand on a metal plate and jump off. She would hang in the air by the two ropes until her team safely lowered her to the ground.

The instructor asked one participant at a time to stand before the pole. Harnessed and ready to climb, she had to name a fear that the pole represented. Then the instructor asked her, "What is the goal you would leap toward if you no longer had this fear?" The participant would answer and then begin her climb.

Most of the participants had to wrestle with some fear about climbing the pole. The energy that surged around this challenge was powerful and connected each girl and adult to emotions they had not been aware of before this moment.

Throughout this challenge, the climbers—adults and daughters—had to decide to move through fear or to stop climbing. The choice was entirely the climber's. Success meant either feeling safe enough to stretch forward and keep climbing or recognizing the unsafe feeling and knowing when to stop.

During the Leap of Faith, a powerful and significant moment for the girls occurred when it was Jake's turn. The instructor asked him, "What is the goal you would leap toward, trusting and having faith in yourself to reach, if you no longer had this fear?" His daughter Kimberly was shocked when her father answered, "I would like to climb to the top of that pole and jump, but I'm afraid of heights, and I'm pretty sure I can't make that happen."

Kimberly turned to her dad and said, "Dad, I didn't think you were afraid of anything."

Jake looked over his shoulder as the hooks were clipped to his harness and whispered, "Kimmy, I'm scared to death right now, and what I've never told you is that this fear comes from falling out of a window when I was a lot younger than you are today. But I'm going to give this a try."

As her dad put his foot on the spike to take the first step up the pole, Kimberly walked over to him, patted his leg, and said, "Dad, it's OK if you're scared. I'll stay right here and cheer you on."

Jake slowly climbed halfway up and froze. "Can't do this. Just can't do this," he said and climbed down. "Sorry about that, Kimmy. I tried. Hope I didn't embarrass you too much."

Kimberly smiled and said, "No big deal. I just never knew you were afraid of anything. Honestly, nothing."

"Well, now you know. And I'm good with it. Being afraid is pretty natural. Everybody is afraid of something. I just know my limits. I'm pretty sure that pole and I will never be friends." Kimberly's dad gave the group the gift of seeing fear as normal, that even parents feel it at times.

Everyone succeeded that day. The Challenge taught an important lesson to the girls about to step into their teen years: fear is normal, and by naming it, facing it, and understanding it, they take control of it and their sense of self gets stronger.

Part Three: The Blessing

The Blessing is the final part of your daughter's sixth ritual. It creates an intentional affirmation of the significant place she will always have in her family. In the face of your daughter's inevitable struggles with acceptance, loneliness, and feeling "good enough," the Blessing serves to reaffirm her family's unconditional love and recognition of her worth and value to them. This creates a powerful send-off into her teen years. The Blessing symbolizes the sacred container that holds her, stabilizes her, and helps her work through the tensions this transition will bring.

My Family's Story: Reflections

Emmy and Halee had turned the corner to their thirteenth birthdays. Our family had spent the day on a challenging ropes course that took at least half of us way out of our comfort zones. Later that evening, we gathered on the back porch to prepare the final part of their ritual. Too tired and too sore to move, I reflected on how quickly the time had slipped by.

Five years had passed since their first rituals. Life had changed for us as a family, especially for our granddaughters. Emmy and Halee had sorted through a whirlpool of emotions, replaced former passions with new interests, suffered consequences, experienced disappointments, and achieved goals that they would not have imagined possible when they were eight. Their lives were not perfect, nor were they. But more importantly, they had developed into kind, smart, curious girls who valued family and themselves—girls feeling fairly confident about entering their high school years.

Parents, uncles, aunts, cousins, and a soon-to-be stepmom anticipated this time to celebrate Emmy and Halee's final ritual. We had been active participants in rituals over the years, helping the girls learn to define themselves by their inner reality rather than their outer context. Our hope for them throughout the stages of their development was that they would discover their own paths and feel confident enough to travel them as independent, caring adolescents.

Returning to the circle now, we spoke and listened to affirmations, sharing words of wisdom and reflecting on the past five years. It was obvious that not only had Emmy and Halee grown, but our connection to one another had also deepened. As we came to the end of the day, Emmy's soon-to-be stepmom, who not been present for Emmy's first ritual, spoke up to offer a blessing to Emmy. Jade knew about the box in which Emmy kept the items family members had given her at her eighth birthday ritual. She wanted Emmy to have an item that represented her blessing of support and love as Emmy entered her teen years. Jade handed Emmy a beautifully carved wooden box and spoke her blessing:

Emmy, I wasn't present at your first ritual, but I am proud and consider it an honor to be present at many moments after that. This box is a way to capture all the new people in this family in your life, and now in mine. I want to acknowledge and embrace the past but also make a container that will hold the future. The box is like you: natural, unique, and beautifully designed inside and out. It represents a new chapter in your life, with new people and new memories.

When she finished, Jade, who had struggled with understanding how to blend into this family, went over and hugged Emmy. For the first time, Emmy returned the warmth of Jade's love. Silence filled the circle. We witnessed the transformation that takes place when we mark stages of our children's life with rituals that dissolve barriers and tap into the deepest part of ourselves.

The essence of our marking the Return was captured by the final blessing during the ritual. An uncle who was unable to attend the celebration sent it in, and his words speak to the heart of the blessing that all daughters need and deserve to hear as they transition into their teen years. It reminds them that there is always a home—a family they can return to, feel safe with, and reach out to for support, love, guidance, and connection.

A blessing from Uncle Austin:

Hey girls,

The object I am presenting to each of you today is a boomerang. That probably seems strange, but for me, boomerangs have a special and personal meaning, which I hope you will soon understand.

When my mom was the age I am now, she went to Australia to teach high school for two years. After she finished up with her time in Australia, she went on an around-the-world trip with her best friend from the school.

As a kid, I remember playing with a big old boomerang that she had brought back from Australia, which now sits on the bookshelf in our home in Germany. For me, it's a reminder of her and of what I inherited from her.

But today, I think that the boomerang represents much more than that. Now that I'm a father, I've thought a lot about my own childhood. Last summer, I went back to my childhood home, which I had avoided for over a decade because it was the place where my mother passed away. Going back to those places and those memories has been very meaningful for me.

Something that my mother and my father always worked very hard to do—and something I know that your parents and your grandparents work very hard to do—is to make a home, a place that's always there to come back to and to feel safe.

For me, that's what boomerangs are all about. What makes them special is that they come back. Throw a boomerang the right way, and no matter how far it goes out, it will always return.

I think being a teenager is about starting to figure out who you are—not just the things that interest you or the things you are interested in but the things you really believe. That means exploring, and that can take you pretty far out into the world. Sometimes it is very hard, and sometimes you may feel very alone as you try to figure these things out. But I hope you know that, like a boomerang, you can always come home. I can safely say that this family will always be there for you. Whatever happens in life, no matter how far you go, you have a home with your parents, with your grandparents, and with your aunts and uncles.

And so, as you go out into the world and start questioning things and start discovering yourself—something that will hopefully last for the rest of your life—I hope that you will remember this home and that you will know that you can always return. Just like the boomerang.

Practicing the tradition of rituals as part of the life of our family had awakened us to their endless opportunities. Our grand-daughters' final ritual, the Return, allowed us to restate our love, support, and commitment by honoring the importance of their lives in our family and the importance our family has played their future. With hugs and laughter, we ended the season of rituals for our granddaughters.

PART III: What Comes Next?

With your daughter's tween years fully behind her, the teen before you is poised to enter the next stage of her life. She is not perfect, nor are you perfect parents; yet together, you and your daughter have built a solid foundation for her to stand on when life inevitably quakes.

With the incorporation of thoughtful, intentional rituals, you've seen her grow more self-aware and confident. She understands and respects her own choices. She has formed a web of connections made up of wise mentors, good friends, and valued family. She's ready to be more independent, knowing that her family will be there when she finds her normally solid ground to be a little rocky.

Though she's turned thirteen, there is no reason for you to stop using creative rituals to mark new transitions and notable life changes. Each ritual provides an opportunity to help your daughter move into new territory with greater awareness of your lifelong support and her continued growth and development. Family members and close friends can continue to share their wisdom and guidance as they connect and exchange similar life experiences with your daughter, enriching every aspect of the ritual.

The next section describes ways families have used rituals for older daughters, particularly for those families who had not previously used rituals as part of their daughters' lives. It also addresses the importance of nurturing yourself—an essential practice for you that also yields enormous rewards for your daughter.

Chapter 11

It's Never Too Late

I am often asked, "Is it too late to begin a rite of passage or ritual with my daughter if she is older than the ages you recommend?" My response is always, "It is never too late to communicate love, encouragement, and support for your daughter." If your daughter is willing to participate, you can construct the rituals in this book so that they are age appropriate and congruent to your daughter's needs.

The power of parenting lies in creating and reinforcing connections that reflect where you all are now. Rites and rituals are a powerful means to do that, no matter the age of your daughter. I have met many families who decided later in their daughters' lives to incorporate rituals to ease the journey through adulthood. Young women continue to need encouragement, meaning, and direction as they make significant choices for their futures, and these rituals can provide that. In this chapter, I highlight the experiences of Jess, whose parents engaged her in a ritual at age thirty, and Stacey, who experienced her first ritual at age eighteen. These stories illustrate the powerful results that the It's Never Too Late ritual can create for older daughters.

The Meaning of "It's Never Too Late"

Rituals can have never-ending power and influence in a woman's life. The pressures facing women do not cease as they mature and age, and for some women, if the development of their internal sense of self was not strengthened and stabilized during childhood, it is possible they will continue to project their childhood dependency onto relationships—personal or professional.

I have worked with women at every age who appear to be confident and in control of their lives, yet when they sit in my office and share their stories, it becomes clear that the image they project is not congruent with their inner lives.

The February 2015 edition of an American Federation of Labor and Congress of Industrial Organizations report states:

> Women make up more than half of the professional and technical workforce in the United States. While the status for women in the workforce has improved over the last several decades, many women still struggle for equality in many occupations. Women are earning post-secondary degrees at a faster rate than men are, yet a wage gap persists. Some portion of the wage gap may result from decisions women make, personal job preference, or socio-economic circumstances; however, many still face overt or subtle employment discrimination, contributing to continued inequality.[1]

During the past thirty years, I have worked with many young women who voice the above concern. They have worked hard to reach personal and professional goals, but as they transition into womanhood, many report feeling they have to leave their true selves at home when they enter the workforce. Within a short time, they learn they must change themselves or negotiate their values to fit a profile that is not congruent to the self they already struggle to own and value. Not wanting to compromise but fearful of not getting ahead if they don't, they minimize their authority and surrender to systems to secure salaries, pay raises, and equal treatment, leaving most of them stuck and stressed.

Jess's story in this chapter mirrors the pressures many young women experience as they work hard to achieve success and professional acceptance while also longing for ways to express fears and self-doubt.

It is not only girls who need wise elders to help them integrate and normalize all the parts of themselves—the good and the bad, the beauty and the beast, the confidence and the fear—without reservation or shame; adult women need the same support.

The Ritual: It's Never Too Late

As you've learned, there's no right or wrong way to conduct a ritual—it's a matter of what works within your family and for your daughter. This is particularly true when creating rituals for adults. Many families with whom I work find that engaging their daughters in the planning process not only creates a shared experience but also opens their daughters to this new way of communicating. Just as with rituals for tweens, creating a specific ritual related to adulthood can be a profound, relationship-altering experience when all participants are committed to engaging in it.

Jess's Story: Turning Thirty

My husband often told our children that their twenties would be about discovering who they were and what they wanted to do with their lives and that their thirties would be about having the courage to live out what they had discovered. As a result, turning thirty has been an important milestone in our home and in my practice.

Jess was going through a particularly challenging time in her late twenties. Though her family had never previously used rituals, they were open to trying something new. Together we decided that Jess's thirtieth birthday would be an ideal time to introduce her to this tradition. They wanted to use the ritual to support and encourage her at a time in her life when she was frustrated and unfulfilled in the pursuit of professional success. She had made some progress in her career goals, but the people-pleasing aspect of her personality was affecting her professional relationships. We created a ritual to encourage and support her in taking charge of her life rather than letting others be in charge.

Her parents told Jess well in advance the date, time, and location of the ritual. Without offering too many details, her mother checked Jess's comfort level with the ceremony that was planned for her. Four women who were close family friends and had known Jess since childhood were invited. The aim was not to surprise her but to keep a bit of mystery about what would take place.

With Jess's approval, several months before the ritual, the four women—the "elders"—were asked to reflect on what life had been like for them in their thirties, what they had learned about themselves, what guidance or support they wished they'd had, and what wisdom they wanted to offer Jess as she transitioned into her thirties. Each woman was asked to bring an object she was willing to part with that at one time had meaning to her and would symbolize the wisdom she wanted to pass on to Jess.

Jess and her mother greeted the women at Jess's family home, and they sat together in the living area catching up. The chairs were arranged in a close circle. Jess's mother started the ritual with the Japanese tea ceremony, an ancient tradition Japanese women shared when they met together. I often encourage the use of this ceremony, as it creates an atmosphere of quietly tuning into, honoring, and connecting with oneself—a practice that young professionals typically do not find time or energy to do.

In silence, Jess's mother poured tea into a cup. One at a time, each participant took a sip and then offered the cup to the woman sitting to her left. The time spent passing the cup, sipping the tea, wiping the rim of the cup, and passing it on to the next person, going around the circle several times, brought a stillness to the group, calming any anxious feelings and racing minds that had occupied the space.

Jess described this exchange later: "During the tea ceremony, I remember first feeling comforted as I let down my walls from years of living an unbalanced life in a busy city where no one paused long enough to notice—much less care about—what was really going on in my life. Tears came to my eyes when I truly felt seen and acknowledged by each one of these amazing women. It has been rare in the world I live in, especially since I became an adult. How often do people come and go in your life, giving and asking without taking time to stop and really see you? Beginning my birthday celebration in this way was awkward for me at first but soon felt comforting."

After the tea ceremony, each elder gave Jess the gift she had chosen for the occasion. With the gift, each shared her wisdom and thoughts that encouraged Jess to succeed by truly being herself. They told personal stories of courage, feelings of inadequacy, and strength that had pushed them through hard times and opened them to new storylines in their lives. One elder gave Jess a fairy holding a crystal ball. She explained that when she was a young woman herself, she had collected fairies. This one was special because her husband had given it to her when she was in her thirties. Handing the fairy to Jess, she said, "Fairies symbolize youthful imagination and an exuberant wonder for life. I encourage you to hold onto your dreams and believe you have the potential to make them come true."

Jess's mother gave her the conductor's baton she had used while conducting a small musical ensemble while living abroad. She shared her hope that Jess would conduct her life as a symphony of music that expressed balance, beauty, and brilliancy. The baton was a reminder that she held the responsibility of choosing the people, partners, and professions that together would create the music to which she would dance and live out her life.

When asked to reflect on her experience of the ritual, Jess wrote:

> Each gift came with words of encouragement and a belief in my abilities to create success and happiness. Not to have the best job or the best husband or the best house, not the equations of society that add up to comparing your soul to an unachievable yardstick—no, they reminded me to believe in myself and to take charge of how I want to orchestrate my life. This ritual gave me the opportunity to look back into my childhood and adolescence and begin developing an image of the woman I want to become. As each of these women shared lessons they had learned, I was encouraged to own all the parts of myself and trust that they represent beautiful and intricate threads that, when woven together, make up the powerful and wise woman I am. Once again, I was reminded that my strength is in my wholeness, not in what I have accomplished or who I impress. When the ritual came to a close, I felt softer and more connected to myself

than I had been in several years. I was ready to return to my busy life and my complicated workplace but far more aware of how little it defined or owned me.

Rituals can also help heal family relationships, no matter your daughter's age. If you are like me, you remember moments as a parent that, in hindsight, you wish you had responded to differently. Although you can't redo those times, you can heal hurts and make different choices in the future. Rituals can help that process.

Often, the mistakes parents make are directly related to their own childhoods. Take a look at what triggers your reactions to your children and what defines your expectations; the insights you gain can build a more stable and enjoyable relationship with your daughter. In their book *Parenting from the Inside Out: How a Deeper Self-Understanding Can Help You Raise Children Who Thrive*, Daniel Siegel and Mary Hartzell suggest the following:

> Contrary to what many people believe, your early experiences do not determine your fate. If you had a difficult childhood but have come to make sense of those experiences, you are not bound to re-create the same negative interactions with your own children. Without such self-understanding, however, science has shown that history will likely repeat itself, as negative patterns of family interactions are passed down through the generations.[2]

Your daughters need your help believing in themselves, knowing that their self-worth is internal, not external, and knowing that you love them and are always there for them. This is true whether they are tweens or adults. But it's not just your daughters who become more whole through rituals—you do, too. Stacey's story illustrates how a ritual can be as healing to an entire family as it is to the daughter for whom it is created.

Stacey's Story: Leaving Home

Andrea created a ritual for her niece, Stacey, who had just turned eighteen and was heading to college. Andrea wanted to remind her how much she was loved and supported as she entered this new stage in her life. She explained later: "From my own experience in college, I knew there would be days Stacey would be homesick and would have doubts about her ability to work through the new pressures as a college student. Although she was ecstatic to try life as an independent eighteen-year-old, I also knew she would struggle to feel capable of doing that successfully. During those times, I wanted her to be able to tap into the memory of this ritual and draw strength and courage from what she experienced."

This was a family in which the girls, including Stacey's aunt, had learned to hide painful and negative emotions to avoid conflict. They learned how to pretend that life was always good, to never rock the boat in fear of tipping Stacey's grandfather into another depression, so despite currents of discontent and disappointment beneath the surface, the family smiled and pretended that all was well.

Andrea said: "By the time I was forty, I had grown weary of living this way. The superficial gatherings our family had become skilled at crafting profoundly shaped how we interacted with our own families, including spouses, nieces, and nephews. So when we explored ways to celebrate Stacey's eighteenth birthday and graduation, I thought of rituals I had learned about at a workshop with Dr. Fleshood. I knew making this happen would be a challenge for our family, but it was one I was willing to risk. This was the perfect opportunity to cultivate meaningful connections in our family. This was my *carpe diem*, and I was going to go for it!"

Since it was her idea, Andrea offered to be in charge of the ritual. Several months before Stacey was to leave for college, Andrea invited the family—parents, siblings, grandparents, cousins, aunts, and uncles—to her home for a cookout. She asked each of them to bring a small gift for Stacey that would serve as a reminder of their support while she was away. The gifts, she explained, should commemorate a special memory or symbolize what the person's relationship to Stacey meant to him or her.

"The idea was that each of us would put a simple, token gift for Stacey in the box I had purchased and briefly describe its significance. Then whenever Stacey felt discouraged or alone, she could pull out her box of family gifts and remember how special she is. I hoped these would give her the confidence to forge through tough days."

After dinner, one at a time, each family member presented his or her gift to Stacey, explained why it was chosen, and told a short story to explain its significance. Not surprisingly, at first the sharing consisted of lighthearted, sometimes humorous, impersonal comments. It was obvious they were not at ease with this new family dynamic.

Then, out of the blue, Stacey's father—typically the least expressive person in the group—stepped forward. His hands did not hold a gift, but he stretched out his arms in an awkward effort to pull his daughter close him. For a family that never expressed emotion, this was foreign and uncomfortable behavior, even for Andrea. She recalled, "I thought to myself, 'Where is the gift? Talk about the gift you have for your daughter! Do something!'"

Instead, Stacey's dad looked into his daughter's eyes and said, "Stacey, I thought a lot about what I wanted to bring to you today.

The gift I wanted you to remember when you were far away study-ing, without any of us near you, is myself. I know we haven't been as close as you might have wanted, and I haven't always supported you when you needed it the most, but I want to do that better in the years to come. So, the gift I leave with you is the memory of me holding you." For what seemed like eternity to those present, Stacey's dad held her while tears streamed down their faces. The room was silent.

When an uncle cleared his throat in discomfort, Stacey's dad dropped his arms and spoke again. "Stacey, I want you to remember when you get in hard places or have accomplishments you want to share that I am here to lean on and to talk with. But most of all, I want you to remember these words: I love you."

Andrea talked later about the significance of that event: "Among a group of people who had learned that being emotional meant weakness, shame, and unpredictable outcomes, in that moment, there was not a dry eye among us. For the first time, a family mem-ber had risked something—and I was later to learn that it was the first time Stacey had ever heard her father say he loved her.

"If it was only for a day, each of us was touched and connected to one another in a way our family had never experienced before. I don't know what impact those moments will have on Stacey, her father, or our family, but they convinced me that I could never return to our old habits of avoiding what is real and meaningful—no matter how uncomfortable it makes us."

Rituals are a sacred exchange between you and the important young women in your life. They allow you to take charge of the relationship rather than staying victim to its history. Even if you feel resistance, know that it can bring freedom from and acceptance of regrets and mistakes that do not have to hold you or your relationship with your daughter captive, nor do they have to be passed down to other generations.

It is never too late to create rituals to mark turning points in your daughter's life. For some families, as for Stacey's, integrating rituals into the family system or into your own relationship with your daughter can be a radical shift in how you relate to one another. If that is the case, see it as an opportunity, not a threat. With patience and perseverance, you can reconnect and rewrite the relationship with your daughter, no matter her age. And for every family, these rituals are a means to demonstrate unconditional support—something that your daughter will never grow out of, no matter her age.

Chapter 12

Seeing Through a New Lens

I was waiting to board a plane when I noticed an overwhelmed young couple with three little girls, passports falling from their hands, backpacks dangling from their shoulders, and snacks crumbling onto the floor. The girls poked at each other, obviously overstimulated and exhausted.

A neatly dressed woman smiled at the couple and said, "You think this is bad now? Just wait until they are teenagers!"

The couple returned the smile and the father playfully responded, "Don't tell them that. Our girls think being a teenager is going to be fun, and their mom and I want to believe that, too."

The lens the woman looked through, framing the teen years as something to dread, was quite different than the father's lens, which showed hope for the future of his three daughters.

Choosing the lens through which you see and experience life requires wisdom and a desire to evolve. Just as your daughters go through stages in their passage into adolescence, so do you grow as parents, changing the ways you nurture, guide, and support your children.

"Yesterday I was clever, so I wanted to change the world. Today I am wise, so I am changing myself." Those words by Rumi, a thirteenth-century Persian poet, helped me change the lens through which I was viewing my daughter. Understanding I needed to clear the lens was a humbling "Aha!" moment for me. I realized that I was projecting the view of life I had when I was young onto my daughter and that it would restrict the development of her greatest self. As a result, she was suffering the consequences of my childhood and not thriving in hers.

From the time she was a toddler, I made sure my daughter's clothes, shoes, buttons, and bows were color coordinated. Coming out of a chaotic family life, my inner life was filled with anxiety and insecurity. I learned early on to do my best to control outcomes, so I began to control my outer world to make it look perfect. With that perspective, I projected my attitude onto the way my daughter dressed. This caused tension, resistance, and tears at an age when Beth was beginning to realize she had her own opinions and, developmentally, needed to assert them in our relationship.

I wanted everything to match, and Beth insisted that orange looked beautiful with magenta. I failed to understand that the way she saw color was through a different lens than my childhood one. Her perspective had limitless possibilities, mine only one: to look good and please others. My illusions that dated back to my childhood were making it difficult for Beth to live her life fully through her own lens.

Beth's Story

One morning, Beth came down to breakfast, ready for school, wearing a multicolored, flowered shirt, striped tights that would look appropriate at a Halloween party, and a purple polka-dot vest. Her face was bright, eyes glittering with satisfaction and confidence.

"Isn't my outfit awesome?" she asked with an authority that left no room for question. "It just fits me, don't you think, Mama?" I stood, stunned, with a coffee mug clenched between my hands, thinking, *Surely you aren't going to school looking like that?* I smiled carefully and remained silent. My rational mind knew Beth needed me to share her excitement, but before I knew it, the wrong words slipped out of my mouth. "Hmm, sweetie, you did a super job, your hair looks great, and you seem to be so proud of yourself." *So far, so good.* But I couldn't let my need go. "But sweetie, do you think those colors really go together?"

Before the last word dropped from my tongue, the sparkle of confidence in her eyes disappeared. In a voice now absent of joy and conviction, her words drifted into a soft whisper: "Mama, if you want me to go and change my outfit, I will. But do you think that maybe we see colors differently, and just for today, can my colors be OK?"

Tears filled my eyes, my grip on my cup eased, and my heart softened in the face of this young girl who longed for her mother to join with her in owning her identity. In the whisper of those few words, my entire body shifted inside, and I knew that the lens through which I saw color would never be the same for me. My daughter, in the wisdom of a creative, loving eight-year-old, released the tight grip I had on what was right for her.

In the months that followed, I realized that my need to control collided with my daughter's need to explore and exercise her independence. My resistance to her owning her opinion in spite of my displeasure would not provide the garden in which she could plant her identity and cultivate her autonomy. My daughter deserved the limitless possibilities that were within her reach and a family who would guide her to them.

As girls strive to successfully differentiate in the midst of their parents' struggle between letting go and holding on, there is a natural tension. In my situation, my need to control the outcome alienated me from supporting my daughter's need to exercise her independence.

It wasn't easy for me to create more space and freedom for the creative and fearless images that were beginning to define my daughter's personality. After all, Beth believed and trusted that she could do and be anything she dreamed, while I was wrapped in fears that limited my potential. I realized my work was to open myself to explore the world through her imagination, letting go of my preconceived notions about what *should* be and instead allowing Beth to take more responsibility in directing who she *wanted* to be.

My work with parents and girls has convinced me that you, the parents, have the power to shift your behavior, your attitudes, and ultimately your daughter's narrative if you are willing to evaluate what isn't working and take a new approach. Seeing your daughter's behaviors and needs through a different lens empowers you both and shifts the currents of your relationship.

Now is the time to change the negative cycle. You can't alter the profound and important brain development that occurs throughout your daughter's adolescence, nor would you want to. You can't eliminate the uncertainty their developmental growth evokes. But you can harness this time and opportunity to powerfully influence a different outcome. A statement that is often attributed to Albert Einstein says, "We cannot solve our problems with the same thinking we used when we created them." The power behind change is motivated by the belief and understanding that things can and should be different.

Throughout adolescence, girls need a platform on which they can evolve as heroes of their own lives rather than falling victim to the lives around them. They need you to use a new lens through which you decide what experiences nurture, prepare, and stabilize their coming of age before they arrive at its front door. If they experience success and develop knowledge of themselves during their preteen years, there is less likelihood of their abandoning their truth when they enter the crises that their teen years will put before them.

Marking your daughter's passage into adolescence with meaningful rituals is a powerful place to start writing your stories. Being the change you want to see defies the long-held myth that has defined and shaped female adolescence as difficult and traumatic—a time in which parents can only hope to survive rather than thrive. Choosing to see through a lens of goodness in the midst of difficult times and view change as an adventure to engage with, rather than restrict, builds bridges that support your daughter as she crosses the great divide between her tween and teen years.

Choosing to be your daughter's companion, guide, and teacher as she walks into this season of her life is a sacred responsibility. Nurture yourself as you nurture her. No parent can be totally sure of how the years will unfold; we can only offer our best and more awakened selves to the process. It is my hope that the stories and wisdom you have found in this book enrich the journey with your daughter and offer insight that opens possibilities for each of you to thrive and reach your fullest potential.

Appendix

The Body Scan

The Body Scan helps individuals pay attention to their bodies. For your daughter, this practice helps her become more aware of how and what she is feeling. As she pays attention to her body and notices anxiety or any emotions or sensation, she learns to observe it without judgment. She has compassion for what she is feeling rather than rejecting it or being upset about it. If she notices anxiety in her body, she can move her focus and imagine her breath relaxing and warming that area of her body. When she becomes aware of painful feelings, sensations, or emotions, she can redirect her attention to another part of the body, intentionally making a choice to stop and try another time or to talk to someone about the feelings.

Set the Stage

1. Find a comfortable place, preferably one where you can lie down on your back undisturbed for about twenty to thirty minutes.

2. Play soft, relaxing, meditative music (without words) in the background. Music is not necessary, but teens often find it helpful.

3. Dim the lights if possible.

4.   Close your eyes. Let your feet fall apart and your arms rest along your side.

5.   Allow your body to get comfortable.

Instructions

1.   Start by bringing your focus to your breath. Imagine the breath as a soft light or a gentle ocean wave moving up through and then out of the body, just as a wave moves up onto the shore and then gently back out into the ocean.

2.   Be aware and relaxed and gentle with yourself. Notice what your body is feeling without any judgment. Begin to notice the surface beneath you and how it feels against your body.

3.   Your mind may begin to wander to thoughts about what you need to be doing or to judging the exercise to be silly and feeling embarrassed. If that happens, notice the thoughts and invite them to leave you alone for now. Then return your focus to your breath moving slowly up through your body and out.

4.   Starting at your feet, focus on each toe, the bottoms of your feet, the tops and the heels of your feet. Think of all the work your feet do for you throughout the day, while playing sports, dancing, or walking the halls. Become aware of how grateful you are for all your feet do throughout the day.

5.   Continue to bring your awareness from your feet to your legs. Notice any discomfort, tiredness, or tightness in your legs. Imagine your breath moving through and around your legs, relaxing them. Let your legs relax until they seem to sink into the surface that is holding you.

6.   Focus on your breath moving up your spine, circling each vertebra, warming the muscles and moving up to the shoulders. Notice if your shoulders are tight or feel heavy. If they

are, simply notice and focus on your breath relaxing your back and shoulders. Notice if there are any messages in this heaviness or stress.

7. Move your breath now to your belly. Notice how it rises and falls with the breath. Notice any feelings or sensations in your belly. Notice and allow the breath to relax the belly, accepting your belly and your body just as they are.

8. Now move your breath from the belly to the chest and the heart. Resting the breath in the heart area, begin to notice what comes up. (Emotions, feelings, sensations?) Allow yourself to be curious, not judgmental, noting any thoughts or feelings that come. Imagine your heart fully opening and letting criticism, self-doubt, and judgment go, releasing them from your heart and beginning to replace them with acceptance, understanding, and love.

9. Gently focus your breath on your face. Notice your cheeks, nose, lips, forehead, and eyes. Let the breath relax your forehead and eyes. Breathe freely, without any control on your part.

10. Now imagine your breath moving to the top of your head, relaxing your mind, your thoughts, and your body, experiencing yourself calm.

11. Allow the breath to begin moving from your head back down through your entire body, slowly relaxing every organ, every cell, every part of your body . . . all the way to your toes. Feel relaxed and calm as you move back down through your body, exploring any sensations in your muscles or skin, your body resting without you doing a thing.

12. With each breath, imagine yourself accepting your body as it is in this moment. Take a moment to thank all the parts of your body for the hard work they do in keeping you alive

and healthy. Notice how you are breathing, how you are resting with each breath.

13. Now begin to shift your awareness from within your body to the outside of your body. Gently open your eyes and notice your surroundings. Slowly move your toes and your fingers and begin to feel the surface beneath you.

14. When you feel ready, sit up and take a moment to notice what you feel and are aware of. Make note to take this awareness with you into the rest of your day and the rest of your life.

15. Allow five or ten minutes to shift from the Body Scan back into the surrounding environment.

Notes

The chapter notes are the result of many years of research, thoughts, and personal experiences of many individuals who have given valuable insight that helped my work come to life. I thank each of them for the wisdom offered to the creation of this writing.

Introduction

1.   Whyte, "Edge of Discovery."

Chapter 1

1.   Mead, *Coming of Age in Samoa: A Psychological Study of Primitive Youth for Western Civilisation*, 10.

2.   Ibid., XIX.

3.   Gilligan, Rogers, and Tolman, *Women, Girls & Psychotherapy: Reframing Resistance*, 105–115.

4.   Pipher, *Reviving Ophelia: Saving the Selves of Adolescent Girls*, 19.

5.   McGrath, "Teen Depression—Girls: How to Get Closer to Your Teenaged Daughter and Prevent Depression."

6.   Shain, "Suicide and Suicide Attempts in Adolescents."

7.   CBS News, "Girls' Suicide Rates Rise Dramatically."

8.   McGrath, "Teen Depression."

9.   Pipher, *Reviving Ophelia*, 13.

10. Puente, "From the Sandbox to the Spa."

11. *The Week*, "Walmart's 'anti-aging' makeup for 8-year-old girls."

Chapter 3

1. Campbell, "The Hero's Adventure."

2. Olson, "Fish Guts and Pig Intestines: Rites of Passage for Adolescent Girls."

3. Mead, *Coming of Age in Samoa*, 136–137, 160.

Chapter 5

1. House, "The Wizard of Oz and the Path to Enlightenment."

2. Campbell, "The Hero's Adventure."

Chapter 6

1. Siegel, *Brainstorm: The Power and Purpose of the Teenage Brain*, 33–34.

Chapter 7

1. Pipher, *Reviving Ophelia*, 293.

2. Hollis, *The Middle Passage: From Misery to Meaning in Midlife*, 23.

Chapter 9

1. Siegel, *Brainstorm*, 2.

2. Ibid., 6.

3. Lantieri, *Building Emotional Intelligence: Techniques to*

Cultivate Inner Strength in Children, 15–16.

Chapter 10

1. Hollis, *The Middle Passage*, 24.

2. Erikson, *Identity: Youth and Crisis*, 92.

Chapter 11

1. American Federation of Labor and Congress of Industrial Organizations, "Women in the Professional Workforce."

2. Hartzell and Siegel, *Parenting from the Inside Out: How a Deeper Self-Understanding Can Help You Raise Children Who Thrive*, 1.

Bibliography

American Federation of Labor and Congress of Industrial Organizations Department for Professional Employees. "Women in the Professional Workforce." Updated February 2015. http://dpeaflcio.org/professionals/professionals-in-the-workplace/women-in-the-professional-and-technical-labor-force

Baum, L. Frank. *The Wonderful Wizard of Oz*. Chicago: George M. Hill, 1900.

Beck, Renee, and Sydney Barbara Metrick. *The Art of Ritual: A Guide to Creating and Performing Your Own Rituals for Growth and Change*. Berkeley, CA: Celestial Arts, 1990.

Bolden, Tonya, comp. *Rites of Passage: Stories about Growing Up by Black Writers from around the World*. New York: Hyperion Books for Children, 1994.

Brizendine, Louann. *The Female Brain*. New York: Morgan Road Books, 2006.

Campbell, Joseph. "The Hero's Adventure." By Bill Moyers. *Joseph Campbell and the Power of Myth*. Apostrophe S Productions. June 21, 1988.

CBS News. "Girls' Suicide Rates Rise Dramatically." The Associated Press, September 6, 2007. http://www.cbsnews.com/news/girls-suicide-rates-rise-dramatically/

Deak, JoAnn. *Girls Will Be Girls: Raising Confident and Courageous Daughters*. New York: Hyperion Books, 2002.

Eliade, Mircea. *Rites and Symbols of Initiation: The Mysteries of Birth and Rebirth*. New York: Harper & Row Publishers, Inc., 1975.

Erikson, Erik H. *Identity: Youth and Crisis*. New York: W. W. Norton & Company, Inc., 1968.

Fleming, Victor, Noel Langley, Florence Ryerson, Edgar Allan Woolf, Harold Rosson, Mervyn LeRoy, Judy Garland, et al. *The Wizard of Oz*. Metro Goldwyn Mayer, 1939.

Friedman, Edwin. *Generation to Generation: Family Process in Church and Synagogue*. New York: The Guilford Press, 1985.

Gilligan, Carol. *In a Different Voice: Psychological Therapy and Women's Development*. Cambridge, MA: Harvard University Press, 1982.

Gilligan, Carol, Annie G. Rogers, and Deborah L. Tolmand, eds. *Women, Girls & Psychotherapy: Reframing Resistance*. New York: The Haworth Press, Inc., 1991.

Gluck, Samantha. "Suicide and Children." Last updated April 9, 2013. Healthyplace.com. http://www.healthyplace.com/depression/articles/suicide-and-children/

Hartzell, Mary, and Daniel J. Siegel. *Parenting from the Inside Out: How a Deeper Self-Understanding Can Help You Raise Children Who Thrive*. New York: Penguin Putnam Inc., 2003.

Hollis, James. *The Middle Passage: From Misery to Meaning in Midlife*. New York: William Morrow, reprint edition, February 20, 2001. Toronto: Inner City Books, 1993.

House, Jeanne M. "The Wizard of Oz and the Path to Enlightenment." *Reverse Spins*. Accessed February 2011. http://www.reversespins.com/wizardofoz.html

Ingpen, Robert, and Phillip Wilkinson. *A Celebration of Customs & Rituals of the World*. Limpsfield, England: Dragon's World Ltd., 1994.

Kabat-Zinn, Myla, and Jon Kabat-Zinn. *Everyday Blessings: The Inner Work of Mindful Parenting*. New York: Hachette Books, 1997.

Lantieri, Linda, and Daniel Goleman. *Building Emotional Intelligence: Techniques to Cultivate Inner Strength in Children*. Boulder, CO: Sounds True, Inc., 2008.

McGrath, Ellen. "Teen Depression—Girls: How to Get Closer to Your Teenaged Daughter and Prevent Depression." *Psychology Today*, June 1, 2002. https://www.psychologytoday.com/articles/200308/teen-depression-girls

Mead, Margaret. *Coming of Age in Samoa: A Psychological Study of Primitive Youth for Western Civilisation*. Perennial Classics Edition. New York: HarperCollins, 2001.

Neale, Linda. "What's the Difference Between Customs, Traditions, Rituals, and Ceremonies?" *Linda Neale and the Power of Ceremony: Linda Neale's Blog*. August 15, 2011. http://www.lindaneale.com/linda-neales-blog-1/whats_the_difference_between_customs-_traditions-_rituals-_and_ceremonies

Olson, Ginny. "Fish Guts and Pig Intestines: Rites of Passage for Adolescent Girls." *YouthSpecialities.com*. September 17, 2009. http://www.youthspecialties.com/blog/fish-guts-and-pig-intes-tines-rites-of-passage-for-adolescent-girls/

Pipher, Mary. *Reviving Ophelia: Saving the Selves of Adolescent Girls*. Trade paperback edition. New York: Ballantine Books, 1995.

Puente, Maria. "From the Sandbox to the Spa." *USA Today*, August 1, 2006. http://usatoday30.usatoday.com/life/lifestyle/2006-08-01-kids-spa_x.htm

Scheer, Scott D., Stephen M. Gavazzi, and David G. Blumenkrantz. "Rites of Passage During Adolescence." *The Forum for Family and Consumer Issues* 12, no. 2 (2007). https://ncsu.edu/ffci/publications/2007/v12-n2-2007-summer-fall/scheer.php

Shain, Benjamin N., and the American Academy of Pediatrics Committee on Adolescence. "Suicide and Suicide Attempts in Adolescents." *Pediatrics* 120, no. 3 (2007): 669–676. http://pediatrics.aappublications.org/content/120/3/669

Shandler, Nina. *Ophelia's Mom: Women Speak Out about Loving and Letting Go of Their Adolescent Daughters*. New York: Crown Publishers, 2001.

Siegel, Daniel J. *Brainstorm: The Power and Purpose of the Teenage Brain*. New York: Penguin, 2013.

Steingard, Ron J. "What Are the Symptoms of Depression in Teenagers? Signs Your Child Might Be More Than Moody." Child Mind Institute. August 25, 2014. http://www.childmind.org/en/postsarticles/2014-8-25-what-are-symptoms-depression-teenagers

Stepp, Laura Sessions. *Our Last Best Shot: Guiding Our Children through Early Adolescence*. New York: Riverhead Books, 2000.

Turkle, Sherry. *Alone Together: Why We Expect More from Technology and Less from Each Other*. New York: Basic Books, 2011.

The Week Staff. "Walmart's 'anti-aging' makeup for 8-year-old girls." *The Week*, January 27, 2011. http://theweek.com/articles/487716/walmarts-antiaging-makeup-8yearold-girls

Willard, Christopher. *Mindfulness for Teen Anxiety: A Workbook for Overcoming Anxiety at Home, at School, and Everywhere Else*. Oakland, CA: New Harbinger Publications, Inc., 2014.

Whyte, David. "Edge of Discovery." Keynote address at the Psychotherapy Networker Symposium, Washington, DC, March 27, 2009.

Wiseman, Rosalind. *Queen Bees and Wannabes: Helping Your Daughter Survive Cliques, Gossip, Boyfriends & Other Realities of Adolescence*. New York: Crown Publishers, 2002.

Acknowledgments

I am indebted to the courageous girls and parents who graciously allowed me to offer their stories to you. Their experiences and narratives have been the cornerstone of my work and the heart of this book.

All narratives develop and unfold because of willing minds and hearts that help to shape them. I particularly thank my three great-spirited and loving granddaughters for allowing me to tap into their lives and experience the depth and healing power that rituals have, not only for those I work with but also for our family.

Cindy Barrilleaux, my brilliant writing coach, editor, and now friend: thank you for the endless hours of encouragement and honest persistence that moved me past my fear this book would never be published to a belief that it would come to fruition.

Amanda Forr is well deserving of my gratitude. Looking at each page of this manuscript through the eyes and heart of a parent of two young girls has been a critical and insightful addition to the editing process. When I thought there were no more words to write, her creative mind reminded me there were.

I am grateful and profoundly blessed by the influence of wise elders—men and women, educators, and spiritual teachers—from the past and present who nurtured my potential, opened me to trust in my dreams, and worked by my side helping those dreams become reality. Thank you for surrounding me with your love and counsel. Your guidance has helped me arrive to where I stand today.

Friends and community who live and walk with me in my day-to-day life are companions I have leaned on and gained wisdom from throughout the writing of these stories. You have been instrumental in helping me accomplish the task of writing this book. I am grateful for your love and especially your laughter.

I am deeply grateful to my publisher, Familius, and to my wonderful editor, Katie Hale. As a first-time author, it has been reassuring to be part of a team process in the final execution of this work. Thank you for valuing my opinions and years of work toward this final product.

Acknowledgment of my gratitude would not be complete without honoring my deepest source of inspiration and joy: my family. Each of you has supported, nurtured, and cheered me on to the completion of this work. Your attention and commitment to implementing rituals in our family's tradition have been an essential and loving contribution to this work. I continue to lean on your laughter, love, and creative minds.

About the Author

MARIA CLARK FLESHOOD is a licensed professional psycho-therapist and a Fellow with the American Association of Pastoral Counselors. She specializes in relationship therapy at her private practice in Virginia, helping couples, parents, and their adolescent daughters maintain meaningful and strong connections.

Dr. Fleshood has been a parenting specialist working nationally and internationally with adolescent girls for more than thirty years. She has counseled adolescent girls and their parents in a variety of private, mental health, and crisis settings. Her academic, clinical, and educational work have led to a creative approach that enables girls to successfully bridge the developmental shift from girlhood to young womanhood. She advocates for a more thoughtful cultural response to this turbulent period of transition in the lives of girls and their families.

Dr. Fleshood has taught in universities and public schools, developed curricula for parenting adolescent females, facilitated workshops and parenting groups, spoken to youth programs, lectured to large groups on parenting female adolescents, and facilitated Mindfulness-Based Stress Reduction clinics for girls. She was trained as a psychotherapist, educator, and theologian. Her multi-discipline approach brings unique insight to her writing and to her parenting methodology.

About Familius

Welcome to a place where parents are celebrated, not compared. Where heart is at the center of our families, and family at the center of our homes. Where boo-boos are still kissed, cake beaters are still licked, and mistakes are still okay. Welcome to a place where books—and family—are beautiful. Familius: a book publisher dedicated to helping families be happy.

Visit Our Website: www.familius.com

Our website is a different kind of place. Get inspired, read articles, discover books, watch videos, connect with our family experts, download books and apps and audiobooks, and along the way, discover how values and happy family life go together.

Join Our Family

There are lots of ways to connect with us! Subscribe to our newsletters at www.familius.com to receive uplifting daily inspiration, essays from our Pater Familius, a free ebook every month, and the first word on special discounts and Familius news.

Become an Expert

Familius authors and other established writers interested in helping families be happy are invited to join our family and contribute online content. If you have something important to say on the family, join our expert community by applying at:

www.familius.com/apply-to-become-a-familius-expert

Get Bulk Discounts

If you feel a few friends and family might benefit from what you've read, let us know and we'll be happy to provide you with quantity discounts. Simply email us at orders@familius.com.

Website: www.familius.com

Facebook: www.facebook.com/paterfamilius

Twitter: @familiustalk, @paterfamilius1

Pinterest: www.pinterest.com/familius

The most important work

you ever do will be within

the walls of your own home.

CPSIA information can be obtained
at www.ICGtesting.com
Printed in the USA
FSOW01n1820050416
18857FS